ODAR
BOOK TWO
SILENCE

Denice Peter Karamardian

ODAR

other; stranger; foreigner
(in the Armenian language)

MEDZ YEGHERN

Great Evil Crime

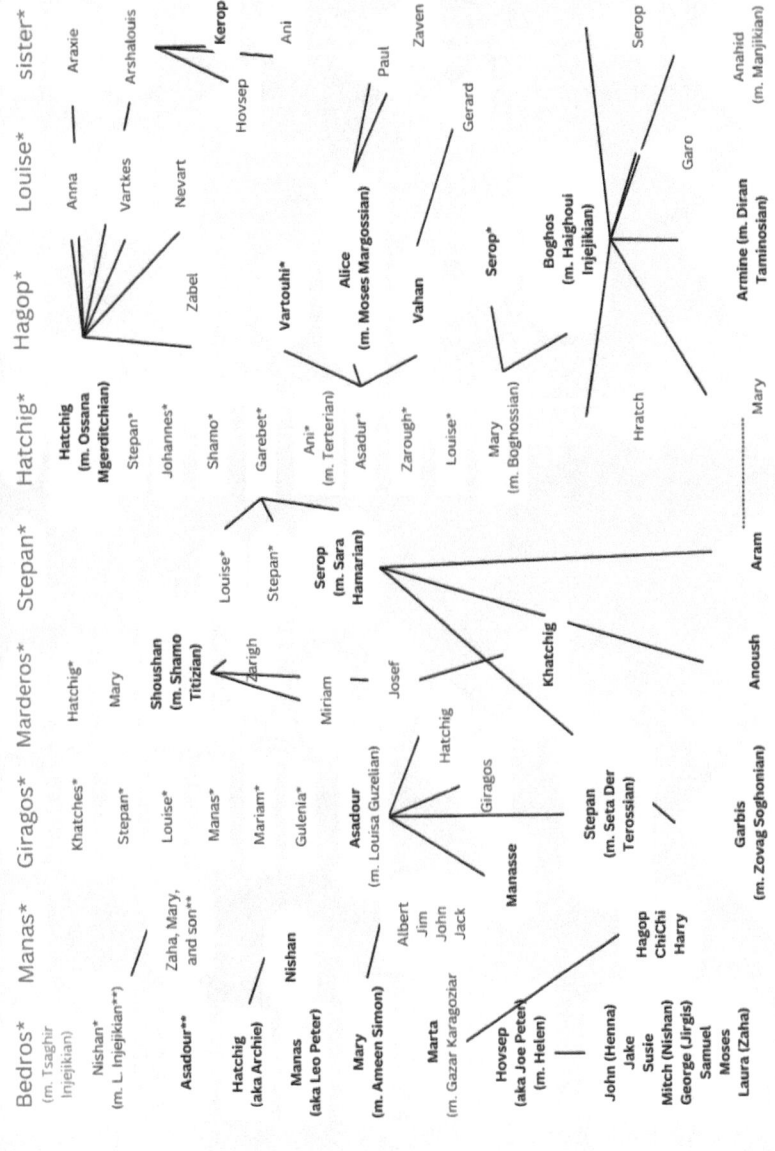

Karamardian family tree approx. 1890 – 1940

*indicates killed or deceased during 1915;

**indicates lost or stolen; names in bold indicates characters in book

Generations Out of Syria

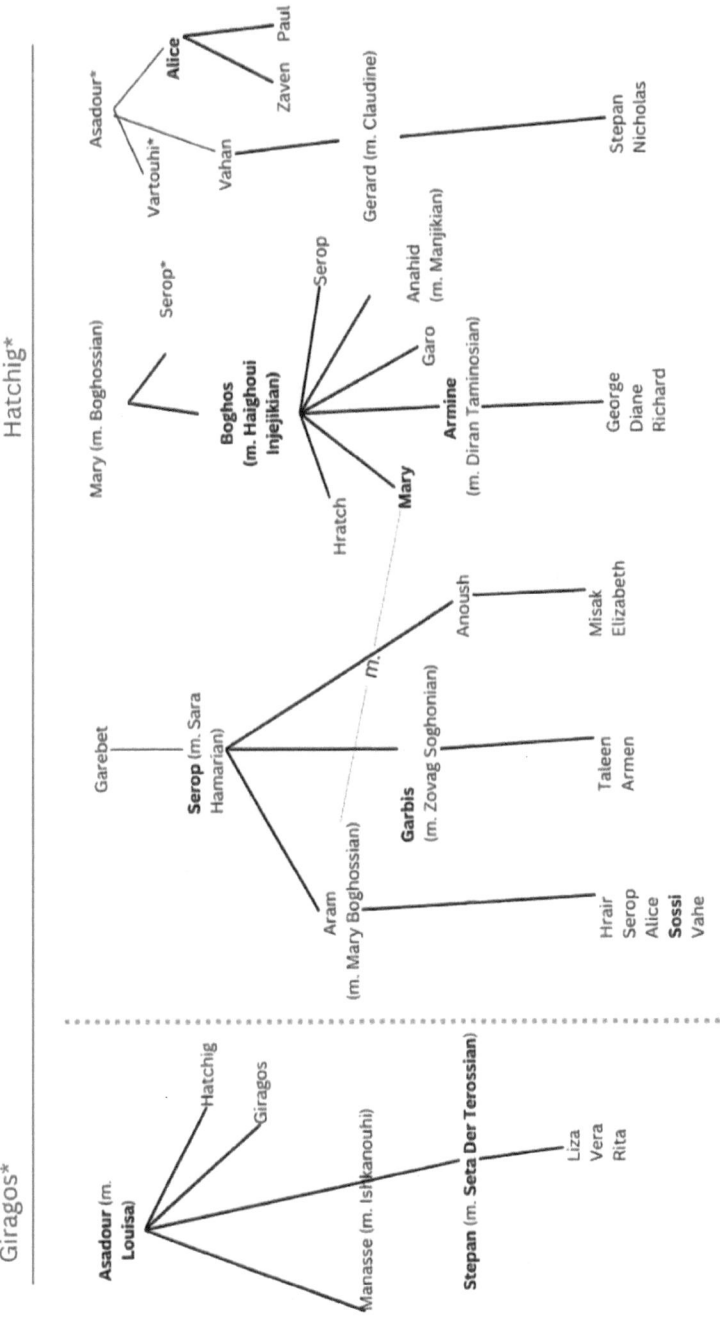

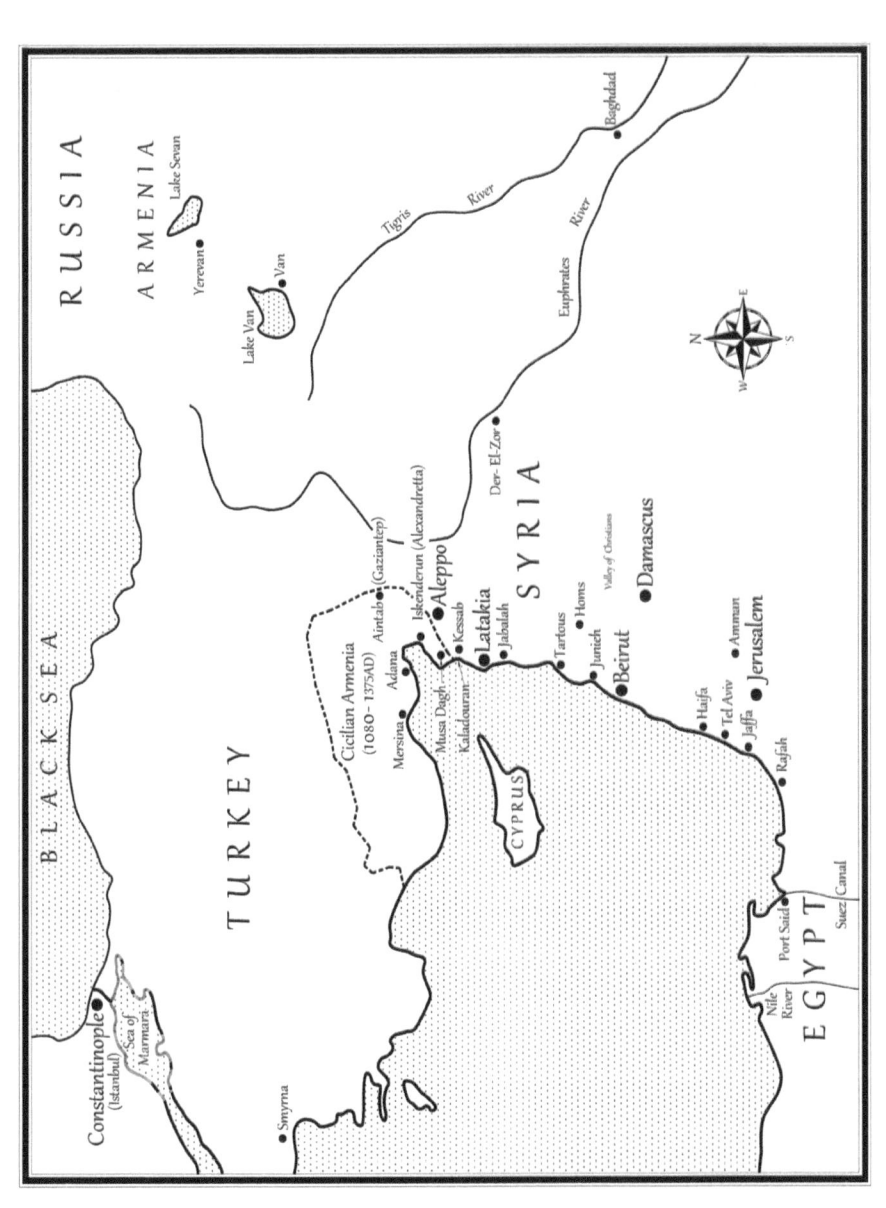

The pomegranate is a symbol of Armenia
signifying fertility and good fortune
and guardian against the evil eye.

"Three pomegranates fell down from heaven: One for the storyteller, one for the listener, and one for the whole world."

...A TRADITIONAL ENDING OF
ARMENIAN FAIRYTALES

For the lost ones....

Copyright © 2024 by Denice Karamardian.
All rights reserved. This book or any portion thereof may not be reproduced or used in any manner whatsoever without the express written permission of the publisher except for the use of brief quotations in a book review.

Publishing Services provided by Paper Raven Books LLC
Printed in the United States of America
First Printing, 2024

Cover image by Sossi Madzounian
Cover design by Kristin Designs

ISBN 979-8-9900982-3-7

TABLE OF CONTENTS

Prologue: Karamardians!..........................i

Chapter 1: Silence 1

Chapter 2: Ameen 9

Chapter 3: Camps 19

Chapter 4: Names 31

Chapter 5: Carts............................. 37

Chapter 6: War.............................. 41

Chapter 7: Legionnaires 51

Chapter 8: Cilicia........................... 63

Interlude: Faces of 1911 73

Chapter 9: Soldiers.......................... 81

Chapter 10: Home........................... 87

Chapter 11: Education....................... 97

Chapter 12: Sister.......................... 101

Chapter 13: Shoe Shop..................... 109

Chapter 14: Land.......................... 121

Chapter 15: Birthing 133

Chapter 16: Community 139

Chapter 17: Gamavor. 143

Chapter 18: News. 151

Chapter 19: Boys 157

Epilogue: Lost and Found. 161

Bedros Line 176

Glossary 179

Bibliography and Recommended Reading 187

Note on Fiction and Truth 191

Acknowledgements. 193

About the Author. 197

PROLOGUE

KARAMARDIANS!

Los Angeles - 1977

AUTHOR

On a sunny August day, I landed at the Los Angeles airport for my very first visit to southern California. At the time, I was living in Denver and about to move to Manhattan to fully immerse in my career. I decided to visit my Aunt Susie before moving back east. I adored Aunt Susie who, quite possibly, was the most outspoken, larger-than-life woman I have ever known. As far as I know, she seldom missed a year of visiting the family in New York until she was well into her nineties with hints of dementia. She came for weddings, funerals, and family reunions (several of these coincided with my birthday and Aunt Susie bought me my one and only Barbie doll). Yet, before 1977, I had never stepped into her life in California.

Under vaulted ceilings overlooking the Pacific Ocean, we stayed up all night in her Rancho Palos Verdes home, chatting like teenagers. In fact, we did this for several nights in a row. She regaled me with stories and details of her life, and we were both surprised when the sun came up and shook us into the day. I'd heard endless stories from sentimental uncles, who had lived raucously and autonomously on the family farm, cocooned in the entitled liberty of "malehood." A glimpse at life in the same family household through the eyes of their big sister revealed a picture so starkly different—she had endured expectations that drastically countered those experienced by her brothers—that she may as well have grown up in a separate household.

"I was responsible for all the clothes. You never saw so many damned dirty pants, socks, shirts, I tell you! And the worst of the chores, too…like the shit wagon…"

I was riveted. Aunt Susie's perception—the eldest girl of an immigrant farming household—flew straight to my heart, and I furiously scrawled notes all over lined notebooks so quickly that they are mostly illegible. I can barely read any of the shorthand I developed on those nights. But I never again looked at anything in the same way, now armed with a new awareness of life for a girl in the same world in which Dad and his brothers had reveled and thrived. Maybe it was then that I began to peer at my ancestors specifically through female eyes.

I had another mission for this trip. Dad had briefly met a man from Kessab at someone's wedding and suggested I pay him a visit. I called Dr. Vahan Churukian, who invited me to his home. A place to begin, I thought, borrowing Aunt Susie's car. This was to be my first interview with a real person from Kessab, who might share basics about the place and what life there was like. I had no expectations beyond this. So, having introduced myself and my connection to Kessab, I was totally unprepared for his first words.

"I knew your grandfather in Kessab. We played together as children…"

I gasped. Time and the air surrounding me came to a halt, however briefly. I desperately tried to absorb the very real concept of Jido *in Kessab*—not only confirmation of his home, but someone's recollection of him from there—long before he existed for me, for anyone in my world. Even as I marveled at this discovery, and mentally barreled ahead gathering questions, I heard, or felt, Dr. Churukian continuing to speak. Aware that I was missing his words, I frantically pulled my thoughts into focus.

"His parents moved to Latakia when we were young, but the family always spent summers in Kessab…" Information was flying at me, too quickly to interject questions. Then, my heart skipped when these words jumped at me: "And I remember the day he disappeared. So suddenly! He was the first to leave."

Dr. Churukian was a vessel of nonchalant statements that poured quietly from his jolly face. Statements that transformed ambiguous information that had been, until now, stored away in my mind as stories: "They put him on a boat in the dead of night, to get him out of the country before it was too late." This sweet man was validating some of the vague fairytales I had lived with! Jido, in a *real* place, a *real* boy playing with friends, "disappearing suddenly" from the community.

But now, Dr. Churukian was still speaking. Pay attention! I silently screamed at myself.

"Oh, and my wife, Sarah," he indicated the small woman who moved on and off the porch, serving coffee and sweets to us, "She is your grandfather's first cousin. Hovsep's mother was

Tzaghir Injejikian, sister to Sarah's father." A name! Tzaghir—my great grandmother!

"Sarah's father, Avedis, was a doctor and the Turks needed him… He helped many of us…" Dr. Churukian was continuing to roll out what seemed random comments.

These revelations were too much to take in at once. I had knocked on his door having no idea what might be achieved. What I was receiving was beyond anything I could have imagined. Overwhelmed, I didn't know where to begin with questions, was trying hard to formulate one, when he said, "You do know, don't you, that you have a cousin here in California?"

I blinked, pulse quickening, and shook my head. What on earth?

"He is Stepan, Dean at Irvine College. His name is Karamardian, too. Dr. Stepan Karamardian. I'll get you his number."

Phone number in hand, I trembled with anticipation all the way back to Aunt Susie's house. I had assumed from all accounts, or lack thereof, that we had no living family, that Jido's family had been eradicated completely, the Karamardian name long disappeared with them.

I dialed the number and a soft voice answered. I stammered out, "Dr. Karamardian? You don't know me but I think we may be related. My name is Denice Peter." The silence felt interminable, giving my mind plenty of time to play every possible trick on me.

He thinks I am a kook, a prank caller, I thought. Oh darn, he probably hung up!

Then I heard him, barely. Almost inaudibly, he said, "Do you have a pen and paper?" I had to ask him to repeat himself and strained to hear.

"You must come to my house immediately. Write down these directions…."

When my aunt and I stepped through Stepan's door an hour later, a whole houseful of people greeted us—a Christmas of Karamardians! Some fifty or more members of an extended family had been called together, evidently gathered in the hour it took for us to drive to Irvine. Stepan was not the only existing Karamardian! Some of the family were recently immigrated from Beirut. My world shifted, standing there in the foyer of Stepan's house, taking in the miracle of family whose existence was unknown to my branch until that moment. Even Aunt Susie was speechless, a rare event indeed.

On that memorable day, I met eighty-year-old patriarch Serop Karamardian, a younger cousin of my grandfather. He had survived the death march to Deir Zor, the worst of all camps in the Syrian desert from where few Armenians survived, even *if* they had managed to reach that final destination. Serop ran a shoe shop in Iskenderun, married, then spent ten years in Brazil operating a shoe shop, before returning to his wife and son. The family then emigrated from Kessab to Beirut where he and his elder son, Aram, operated a yogurt shop. Serop's sons, Aram and Garbis, their wives, Mary and Zovig, and his daughter, Anoush, were now resettled in southern California with their children—the cousins of my generation. Living, breathing cousins with my Jido's real last name! And my first real glimpse at life in the old country. For the tribe.

The walls of Stepan's home were lined with stunning carpets and tapestries. I thought of the contrast on the other side of the country where, in the homes of my uncles and parents, a requisite camel saddle perched beside each fireplace, as was the custom decor of Lebanese and Syrian families in the 1950s and 60s. Wall carpets and camel saddles—familiar items I'd never given any thought to—suddenly represented cultural significance. I was self-consciously aware, even felt myself cringe, when Aunt Susie strode through Stepan's house pointing at, and commenting on, carpets and artifacts in her strong, no-nonsense voice with its lingering upstate New York twang. How jarring her blatant manner might seem to the soft spoken Karamardians, who would never have gushed at 'things.' Clearly, I thought, the lives and personalities of these Armenian relatives were unequivocally different from those of the Syrians and half-Syrian/half-Armenian Peters of New York, to whom I belonged.

Yet, they also felt eerily familiar on some unknown plane of consciousness. I felt especially drawn to the cousins of my age—Sossi, Vahe, and Alice Karamardian—and adored the opportunity to peek at their lives inside a real life Armenian community, something I had neither experienced nor imagined. What was it like, being Armenian? I craved to know. Observing them felt a little like coming home, though not exactly recognizing home. I was a time traveler who didn't belong. As if, it was I who had changed, and not the home.

I spent the next few days in wonder, literally basking in the glow of my new-found family and their community. I visited their homes, their Armenian schools and churches, attended a festival and enjoyed many meals on patios. Dozens of people sat around a table, attempting to hash out a family tree for me by interviewing the elder Serop about names, everyone jumping in to help translate and gently correct one another. Every one of them, blood relatives with a place on the family tree we were fashioning, had been born in Kessab, Latakia, or Beirut. My Karamardian cousins had traded in one world and assimilated, not so much as Californians, but as Armenians in California. I wanted to know what that was like. In that moment in August, 1977, my mind and senses were on steroids and I wanted to soak it all up.

I stayed a few days with Stepan, his beautiful wife, Seta, and three young daughters. Stepan and I celebrated our birthdays, one day apart. Stepan's father was Asadour Karamardian of Kessab, my grandfather's cousin. I was surprised to learn that Stepan knew, for some time, of our family branch, even aware that our name had been changed to Peter. The couple related to me how, when they had visited New York for their honeymoon, they had driven across the state, looking for our last name *Peter* in the fat phone books that hung on chains in the phone booths of the day. They recalled focusing on the city of Utica (rather than Ithaca), repeating my Jido's historical mistake. I instantly fantasized a day in the future when my father might meet Stepan, how they would likely bond. I saw them as parallel pillars of a family legacy, from opposite sides of the "old" world to opposite sides of the "new" country. They represented the soul of a family of which I felt more and more humbled to be a part.

My father stood out among his siblings—all businessmen—in his dedication to higher education (as a trustee and employee advocate), specifically to his beloved Cornell University and to the furtherance of scientific discovery through his career there with the Arecibo Observatory. Stepan, currently a Dean at U.C. Irvine, was in the process of co-founding The American University in Yerevan, Armenia. Both men shared a devotion to education, from lives strikingly different yet containing certain parallels. I began to envision a story highlighting parallel lives of Karamardian branches—in the old country, and the new—and fantasized a shape for this book. When I described my vision to Stepan, he rocked my world yet again. His words spilled excitedly into the air around us, filling the room, my ears, my senses: "Denice, my mother has only recently died. But she left a diary. You see, she was the family historian, she documented everything about the family. She worked for the missionaries. My father helped your grandfather get his sisters back from the Turks and to America, and my mother recorded every detail!"

My heart meter rang off the charts. All of this discovery of family and connections now vaulted to a higher level—the prospect of solving mysteries—a gold strike! My generation had been told wild stories about our great aunts: that they were kidnaped by Turks, taken to Turkish harems (was it an exaggeration?), that Jido and his brothers in America had "bought" them back from the Turks and brought them to the United States. The stories seemed too crazy to be true, and were never elaborated upon with any sort of detail, so there were points in time when one almost dismissed them as fantasy.

But now Stepan was validating the rumors and offering me the best gift of all…details! I fantasized about all those blurry images of the ordeals of Aunt Mary and Aunt Martha, clicking into sharp focus. I also thought about Jido: what did he know (of the horrors he had left behind in Syria) and when did he know it? When was his father murdered?

"You must wait for me to translate her diary for you, in order to write this book."

My joy was two-fold: in anticipation for the true story to be revealed—for that in itself—I was more than content to wait for Louisa's journal; also, a convenient reprieve of time to spare was granted. I was about to move to New York City, quite anxious to dive deep into my theater career, and happily accepted that I must put aside the story until the diary was translated. I swelled with both relief and elation, knowing that the work of the book would come in the right time, aided by the unexpected tool of Louisa's diary. Real facts! I did not imagine a delay decades-long, only the happiness of what there was to look forward to.

Before I left Stepan and Seta, I decided to claim the ancestral name that belonged to me. Back in Denver, as I packed for New York, I added this birthright to the name I'd been born with and officially became Denice Villa Peter Karamardian. And so, at the age of twenty-six, I settled into the Manhattan theater scene armed with my new—or old—identity.

Before I left L.A. though, there was one more surprise—bittersweet—to be had during the California odyssey. When I had planned the trip, I did not know that Uncle Leo, Jido's youngest brother (originally named Manas), was still alive. I was taken aback when Aunt Susie brought him up, and I begged her to take me to meet him. Naturally, she groaned and tried to discourage me. She had already described Uncle Leo's cruel impact on her early childhood, the words still stuck in her head of Leo growling at someone in the household, "I'll give you five dollars to take this ugly one down to the river and drown her!"

Now, her twang turned up a notch, exasperated. "What the hell good can Leo do for you?"

But I ignored her disdain (was it pain?) and persisted. I knew well that grudges ran deep in our family. But although she'd faithfully nursed her resentment and had had nothing to do with him for many years (which might explain why she was unaware of living, breathing Karamardians right under her nose in L.A.), she reluctantly gave in to my plea. Leo lived in an old section of Hollywood. We found him bedridden, inside a dim and dingy apartment that we climbed several staircases to reach. An elderly woman cared for him and I never knew, or asked, who she was: caregiver, wife, nurse? She served us tea and water. Leo's appearance was shocking, his body small and frail (and harmless). I had not worked out questions that I could have asked but, having just learned from Dr. Churukian that Jido's family had, at some point, moved to Latakia, I started there.

"I was still very young when we moved, but I remember suddenly having to learn Arabic…" His voice was so weak and soft, I strained to hear. "…I recall a grandfather coming to visit us, and many uncles, especially four of them. Giragos was my favorite…."

Five decades later, I know some of the names! So I know now that the visiting grandfather would have been either Khatchig Karamardian, father of Bedros, or Gabriel Injejikian, the father of my great grandmother, Tzaghir. And the names of many more, scratched onto the family tree in my notebook.

I managed to ask what he could tell me about his brother Asadour.

"Hovsep and Asadour were denied entry to the U.S. because Asadour's eyesight was defective," he mused and mumbled something about ending up in the islands. Then, "He went to South America. I heard from him twice, the last time asking for money."

My grateful heart rejoices for the few words he spoke and the even fewer notes I jotted down that day, though I'll forever regret not having scrawled more detail, for Uncle Leo passed away two months after my visit. Little did we realize how close he was to death. Ironically, it would fall to Aunt Susie to attend to arrangements for his burial.

Evidently, he had no one else.

CHAPTER 1

SILENCE

Highland Park, MI - 1914

HELEN

I glance over at the silent woman at my sink. Sounds shove their way in from the window, never letting up, especially now that the sash stays open throughout the day. Clacks of iron horseshoes on the street, airy pops of car horns, the occasional screech of the streetcar. My husband harbors a strong aversion to city life and yet, here we are. Back at Henry Ford's big company with everyone else: there is no shortage of work for the masses of people who flock to this place. It is summer and the streets are always filled with people calling out in languages from Arabic to Slavic. The sounds. Do they invade her senses as they do mine?

She has come, Mary, and stays with us. Yussef has moved us back to Highland Park. With savings from the farm produce, he bought this house on Cottage Grove, just around the corner from where the brothers still reside on Kendall. Yussef says we will return to Port Hune before long, where I know he prefers to live and work at the salt company because he can make extra earnings on the farm we rent there. But it galls him to pay rent, a waste of his time and money, so he says earning rent from this house after we leave Highland Park will offset that loss. It can't be soon enough for me.

I consider Port Hune our home now. We have friends, and the priest, there. My brother has finally found a suitable house in Port Hune and secured a shift at the salt block. I sincerely hope that he holds onto it since his new bride, Mary, has a young one now. Strange that we have abandoned them just when they can use some family in their new lives. But Yussef works now for Ford, along with the Simon brothers, and says we will stay until after the wedding. I am busy with Henna and the new baby, Jirgis; he is so fragile for four weeks old, unlike my first. We are okay, for now. But I am at a loss with this new member of the family, a stranger at my sink.

She says nothing, this sister of my husband! I can see she is exhausted. She stands most of the day by the stove seeing to the shadiyeh (pilaf), to which she adds lentils or sometimes pine nuts—she says it's the Armenian way—and tomato lamb stew, while I tend to the babies. She has already adapted to the modern stove of Amirka. But no matter the kind of fatigue that traps her, she holds her head in a proud way. I was not prepared for her beauty, nor her… attitude. It is not that I had any expectation; whatever could I imagine from such a victim of bad luck or fate? But she is strangely silent, and well, maybe a little haunted. At times she stares out the window like she is dreaming. What goes on in her head? I would trade my mother's candy dish that I carried all the way on the big ship across the oceans to read her head or hear things tumble from her lips.

For that matter, whatever goes on in the minds of my husband and his brothers? An arranged marriage? P'sh! They seem to have bargained for her escape, snatching her from one slavery only to sell her off! Well, that's my opinion and I tried to bring it up. Yussef would not have any of it.

"You do not know about it, Haloun! Leave it be," he snapped in the way that closes a topic for good.

I believe I can guess what they think: they assume she is damaged goods. But who can know anything of her? She has shut it down. There are moments I steal glances at her frozen face—stuck in time or who knows what—and I wonder if she will ever share her experiences with another. No. I feel in my gut that she will take what she endured to her grave. It is no fault of her making. And now, her life is still not hers to choose. Strange, though, she shows no sign that she is bothered by it. Maybe she is relieved and grateful? Perhaps the Simon family is safety for her; after all, they initiated her rescue. Hah! And got a wife for Ameen in the bargain!

But is it right? I would never have it. Would my brother have dared to do this to me? I think not. Even had he tried…

Well, for now she has four months of freedom. Free to be silent in my kitchen. It is so hard to work by the side of a mute woman.

I am not even sure my husband knows his sister at all. I suppose she was just a girl when he left the old country. I believe Manas was closer to her; for him, Mary is a goddess. He spoke of her often during the months he laid on our sofa in Tubbha, of her unusual beauty. That much is true. Funny, though, when she first arrived and they laid eyes on her, all three of them seemed afraid and shy of her. They embraced her tentatively, like they feared they would break a doll. I cannot imagine their home life to have been without passion; but maybe it was the fact that—or shame that—they had not protected her and cannot know what she has suffered. And she, the eldest female, managing the family. Who can imagine?

The mystery is getting to us all.

I must say, to see them baking side by side in the kitchen, Yussef and Mary, is a sight few would expect. My husband is a baker; he worked at it in the islands, before he came to New York, and lately at the salt plant in Port Hune. He now tenderly gestures to his younger sister and throws the bread dough into the air to flatten it. She is at the table, rolling up the philo with walnut filling and lays out the wrapped logs on a sheet pan to be drizzled with sugar syrup before baking. Her 'boorma' takes on a different shape than the diamond cut baklava that I learned in Melkia, although she says they make that kind too, in the Armenian and Turkish households. I believe Yussef learned from his own mother how to bake bread. He says Mary was already cooking when he left the old country, though she was just a child. I try to imagine the life for them in a motherless household and I admit it—my heart melts a little toward her, toward them all. Life deals a cruel hand sometimes, and without warning.

"*Inch bes es?*" she asks Yussef when he arrives after work.

To which he replies, "*Shad lav em, park asdouzo.*" (I guess this to be the standard greeting, since it is repeated every day). And so begins our evenings, joined by the brothers.

The four of them murmur together after the supper meal, and I try to listen but I cannot understand many Armenian words. The information they received from Mary about the old country is not happy. I can tell by their eyes, their tone, their heads lowered at certain exchanges, and I wish I could share some of my husband's burden. But when he finally comes to the bed he does not bring it with him. I feel completely shut out. It is not my nature to suffer in silence, let alone stay out of conversation. And so I try to focus on the little ones, my Henna and Jirgis, who fill my days with their constant needs, may God bless them.

There are things to do for the wedding. Mary must have a dress, new and clean. I do not know if it should be white and I dare not ask. We will take her to the city center. Yussef will buy her a dress that I will help her to fit, that is, if Jirgis will allow me a few necessary minutes unattached to my breast. Such a hungry child, and Henna is only just walking a little and must be chased at the same time. My work is chaotic with the two young ones, but Mary helps with Henna, whom she sometimes calls John—the name the Amirkans use—thanks be to Allah. And when she cooks the special dishes from Kessab, the faces of her brothers light up like the firelights we saw by the big lake in July.

That is my favorite holiday, now that I am in my new country four years already. I love the fire explosions, and they come always over a lake! The lake at Tubbha, in Myers, called Cayuga, was long and narrow, fingerlike, indeed. Lake Hune is more like a sea; even Lake Santa Claire is a sea and from the shore, the colorful blasts are something to behold in the dark sky.

The leftover embers drift down like snowflakes to be swallowed by the water. We took Mary there on July 4th, to picnic at the Gross Point Park and watch the exhibition with Leo and Archie. These are the names everyone is calling Manas and Khatchig now. The Simons were also there. Different from the intimate gatherings on Myers shores of Lake Cayuga, this city spits out swarms of people with the same purpose in mind. Yussef said it was like Carnival in the tropics with the festive lightness of the crowds, the vendors, the holiday greetings. The celebration of the new country, he says, is to be our celebration every July! This one in Michigan was real special, filled with people like us, recently arrived in our new land and building our families and lives from the security of real work. It is marvelous to think of. Sometimes I feel part of something so big and endless.

Still, she says so little to me that I am annoyed most days. I would love to be able to chat with someone, to feel the joy of friendship. She absorbs my husband's attention, understandably. But I miss him. And I miss friends. This I am beginning to understand. My cousins Abe and Martha have recently written that they arrived from Syria and live in Geneva, New York. I am too far away to be reunited with them. Also, I very much miss my friend Alice. Her Abraham has opened his barber shop in Ithaca; I would love to see it one day. I even miss my brother Mussa in Port Hune, who everyone but me calls Moses. This city of workers for the driving machine plants is empty of family of my own. And I find it difficult to adjust to Amirkan names. Except I am grown accustomed to my own name Helen, since no one but Eassa Simon utters Haloun at times. This sister-in-law, Mary, pronounces it funny. Eh'len. She leaves off the puff of air that the first letter makes. Perhaps it is the Armenian version, I should not care.

Aieeya, here I am, feeling sorry for myself, and yet... I cannot imagine enduring what this beautiful sister has been made to survive. I am once again ashamed of my thoughts. Yet it is impossible to be of comfort to one who will not receive comfort or any sort of communication. It is maddening. But there is nothing to be done.

CHAPTER 2

AMEEN

Highland Park - 1914

MARY

It is a strange country, this Amirka. But God is merciful that I am here and in the company of my brothers. Khatchig and Manas are a comfort. Hovsep at first seemed like a stranger. He seems to live his life in an Arabic world, removed from his roots by time and distance, while trying to spin that world into an Amirkan one. Not that I blame him for whatever he must do. It is just that he is less familiar to me in this new place and after so long. And why wouldn't he be? He has paved the way for us all and keeps moving forward. I have not yet seen much of Amirka outside the house. All in time. I am patient. I must begin by practicing to use the Amirkan names for my brothers: Arch-ee, Lee-oh, Josef……

Just a few months ago I thought my life over. And here I am, across the world, pushing away critical thoughts of Hovsep's wife as best I can. *Josef's* wife, I remind myself. She is pretty. She is strong and forceful, and I can see that my brother is attracted to her nature. For me, well, she talks non-stop and what I hear from her is gossipy and judgmental, maybe because she has no education. I do not believe she can even read. I do not know what to say to her that she will understand. But mostly, because she is like a gale of wind that will not relent, I fear her questions. I cannot go there, cannot know the answers. So it is best not to encourage conversation. Poor thing. She must feel alone without family or friend. After all, she is *odar* among my brothers.

I am grateful. Truly, I am. The poor thing did not sign up for Hovsep's…Josef's family, though she is certainly hospitable. Here is the thing I have avoided thinking much about: I, too, am about to be passed into an Arabic family. Imagine. What would my family in Kessab think? Hovsep and Manas know the Simons. They have told me what they know, even that the younger brothers had been at the mission school ahead of Manas. When we were introduced, I noticed the cross tattooed on John Simon's forearm and felt at once comforted by this sign of piety in my future parents. Like me, they were born in Ladehkiya. They were part of the missionary network and— I shiver to think of it—they contacted the missionaries who put my rescue plan into action! Were it not for them… then what?

Actually, I might have plotted a plan for my own death by now. But, enough!

I am to marry their eldest son. It seems only fair. He is a mystery to my brothers who are younger than he and have had no relationship with Ameen, even to Hovsep who has known him the longest. I am told he came to Amirka about when Hovsep and Asadour departed from Syria. His family followed in groups of two or three, until all were together at a salt company in New York, where Hovsep met them, and Manas, too. He is employed as a machinist at the company they call Ford. He will provide for me; my brothers say this much is certain.

"I am sorry, Mary. Ameen does not speak much. He was already settled when I arrived at the salt block, and well… he seems quite solitary." Hovsep tried to explain to me why his personality is less known than his parents and brothers. "But he has dignity."

None of my brothers have had a proper conversation with my husband-to-be, in spite of their explanation that Hovsep is close with the father, John, and Manas close to the brothers, Najeeb and Abraham. Ameen is very tall. That is all I noticed when I looked that first time, when they pointed him out. I saw him again, when my brothers and Helen took me to the lake to see fire lights thrown in the sky. With some brief glances I could see that he is pleasing to look at but I could not hear him speak. I do not know if we'll meet again before we are wed in October. I tell myself this: had I been rescued and hidden away in the old country—had I not been brought to Amirka—I could not have married. Who would have me? I would grow old caring for others, no children of my own. But at least I would be seeing to Marta's well-being.

Marta! Oh, my dear little sister, Marta! Will I never see her again?

The days are shortening and the air is brisker. It tells me that winter is on the way, and I am warned by everyone that winters here are much colder than I have known. My wedding is quickly approaching. Hovsep and Helen will return to Port

Hune soon afterward. She talks about it endlessly and is counting the days, although she claims to appreciate this time with an extra pair of hands. They have graciously shared with me their precious home, to see me settled and cared for. For these few months it would not be proper for me to stay with my in-laws before the wedding, nor alone with my single brothers. And so Hovsep, Josef—who is called Joe by all the Amirkans—brought us all to the city to solve the dilemma. It seems that documents on my behalf are also being worked out over the summer months. Everyone has given so much time and effort for my sake and I owe my life to all of them—family here, and the many unknown angels back home. I must repay them with a successful life as Ameen's wife, as mother to John and Mary Simon's grandchildren, and as a secure and self-reliant sister, posing no further burden on my brothers.

I pray for one thing more: that one day Marta will join us in this new world, Detroit, Amirka. I will not mention this yet to Hovsep; my brothers have compromised their lives and may see my hopes as a demand they cannot meet at this time. And I do not know of my husband's nature, assets, abilities, or least of all, his inclination to aid my request. Since I know nothing of him, I am at the mercy of whatever his character may be.

If I were home, I would have a say in any suggestion made to me by Father or Nishan, my eldest brother, regarding marriage. Hah! In Ladehkiya, I would be presented with choices of marrying someone from Kessab or any of its villages; possibly an Armenian from the city though there are few of marriageable age, and even those typically seek a wife from Kessab. But a Syrian would be unthinkable, even a Christian one. Funny, now two of Father's children will be married to Arabs, although Hovsep's union is a love match by choice and not usually considered advisable. Reservations have no place in my mind now. I must prepare my heart for the best, to embrace the family I owe my life to, to be grateful their eldest son is neither elderly nor homely. I have already known the worst and am fortunate for a future.

The ceremony is to take place at the home of the Simons. It will be very brief and followed by the normal plates of light food—dolmas, hummus, lamajoun—that men will eat standing up and women will balance on laps. Helen and I press and prepare the new dress. It is of creamy lace, not quite white but white enough to acceptably pass for appropriate bridal appearance. At least no one will have questions because of it. I was relieved and so grateful to Hovsep and Khatchig for its purchase. I also have brand new shoes, from the shoemaker shop of a countryman. It was difficult to enter the place; I held back tears for my father, my hayrig, until I was in my bed that night. And sweet Helen surprised me with new white stockings. When I thanked her, she told me a dear friend in New York had done the same for her and also seen to it that she had new shoes. She then handed me a ribbon to bind my hair and helped me loop it so that it hangs just below the neck.

When we arrive on Victor Avenue and enter the house, I am overcome with emotions that I cannot sort out in the moment. Is it relief? Is it fear? Am I being swept away out of my own control? I can't place the feelings and so I summon the thoughts I need and determine to supplant all others with these: I am gratefully embarking on my future; I am blessed with a husband who will care for me and seems very level-headed and calm. This suits me. I am blessed with in-laws and new brothers to know, and my own brothers are again in my life.

I allow myself to look directly at my husband now, still as far across the room as that first time when I dared not look. This time, he levels his gaze on me and looks directly into my eyes. He makes a small smile, very small, but enough for me to sense it was meant only for me. This is curious and also relaxes me. Ameen Simon took a chance on me as well, and his smile suggests that perhaps he is not disappointed.

Four of us are summoned to a parlor by a Reverend, a man who reminds me of the kind missionaries at home and who shows us a paper to sign: Ameen and me, and our witnesses. I say my name is Mary Peter, using my brothers' style the way they showed me. Hovsep taught me the words in English for my name and I will learn more later, but cannot write in this language. So the Reverend wrote out for me this name and I place an X next to it. It is only for some minutes more, since I will soon be Mary Simon (like my mother-in-law).

When he comes to the place where the paper says to write names of father and mother, I squeeze my eyes shut for only a second, so no one will notice the pause. I must use the American form of name because I forgot to ask Khatchig how to say Karamardian in English. I tell the man Peter Peters for my father, Bedros. And for my mother, when I realize that I cannot say Tzaghir in Amirkan, I summon up her nickname, Haigha, and he adds Peters. Helen is witness for me and I watch her carefully scrawl an X next to the word Mrs. Peter that Anis wrote down for her. I understand in that instant how she must have practiced the symbol and how my suspicion of her lack of learning is far closer to the truth than I even imagined. Yet, even I am helpless, rendered illiterate in the new language of this land. Ameen's witness is his brother Anis Simon. He is only three years younger than Ameen, and I will come to learn just how close the two brothers are… almost inseparable.

We return to the main room and I allow myself to look about this room, clean and rearranged for the festivity. The table, covered in a lace cloth beneath the platters, is pushed against a wall. I let myself absorb the knowledge that from this moment forward it is my home, a home I will share with this new, large family. I then look to the faces surrounding me, gradually taking my time with one at a time, identifying a new relationship to each set of eyes I meet. It is comforting, this strategy. It removes fear of the unknown and replaces some of the unease I have felt with a deliberate study of the people in my new life.

There are my brothers and Helen, who is enjoying this unique social opportunity away from her kitchen. I glance at Manas—I must remember he is called Leo in this country—and take a moment to hope he maintains his best behavior. My other brothers, Khatchig and Hovsep, also have new identities in the new country. Archie and Joe. I will honor them. My eyes light on John and Mary Simon; brothers Anis, Najeeb, and Abraham; Louise (who is Helen's good friend) and her betrothed William; sixteen-year-old Lula, and eleven-year-old Nadeen.

And finally, Ameen, still watching me.

The ceremony is short. A curious thing happens. At the time for exchanging vows, the minister holds out a Bible for Ameen to place his hand on. But Ameen balks and stammers that he'd like to use his own book. We wait in silence as he rushes out of the room to collect it. When he returns with the book, he glances at his father, then attempts to explain to those of us close enough to hear his soft voice.

"When I left Syria alone, my father gave me this Bible. It is partially translated to Arabic, so that I was able to read it before I gained command of the English. Thank you for your patience." He then murmurs some version of the explanation in English to the minister. These are the first words I have heard from the lips of this stranger, my groom.

When my new husband takes my hand to place the ring, I see the tattoo. It is his name, in Arabic, on the left hand. I wonder if he is the kind of man I can ask the reason or incident that caused this. Perhaps it is not so much of a story, but just the impulse of a young boy. Yet, he showed, through his Bible, that he is powerfully sentimental. I hope he is not closed to conversation. He towers over me, almost six feet in Amirkan inches, I am told. His age is that of our dear Nishan at home, dear God, let him be well. Ameen's eyes are as dark as his hair but are not unkind, like the beady eyes of the Turkish men who imprisoned me. As the ceremony finishes, I feel warmer toward him and I wonder if I will love him. Wouldn't that be an unexpected blessing!

The family has prepared a private room in the house for us. It is the 17th day in October, and Ameen will go to work on Monday. We have only one day to get to know one another and then I will be on my own with this unfamiliar family to forge my way. His voice makes me jump.

"Mary, I hope you will be comfortable at home. My shift each day will be long. Sundays, I am free for worship… and you." His voice is marvelous! His manner and words, educated.

"I will make myself useful." I really could not guess what else to say.

"My God, you are beautiful…" are his last words as I enter the bed.

It is then that I decide I am grateful that he is a man of little talk. Though he must wonder, I am confident he will not ask me questions which cannot be answered about that which is unexplainable. And to ensure that silence, like a contract between us, I will refrain from asking him questions of my own. Praise be to God. Thank you for the blessing of my new life and the protection of my husband. It is clear my life is meant to be what it is. And I will honor it.

The first week with the Simons is as natural as I could have hoped. Nobody pressures me to open up; their natures are more contained and subtle than Helen's. The Simon sister, Louise, just a few years older than I, is comfortable to be with and I will help her plan for her wedding to be celebrated in the coming year. Wide-eyed Lula is a delightful girl and it feels once again like having a little sister in the home. I wish they could meet my Marta. When Ameen and his brothers return from the Ford plant at night, they hungrily eat and remain seated round the table for talk and tea. Eventually, Ameen takes my hand and walks me to our room.

Our happiness is marred before the end of our first wedded week. I weep for dear Helen and Hovsep—Joe! They returned to Port Hune the day after the wedding and were gone just three days, when little Jirgis did not awaken. The child, not yet six months old, died in his sleep on the 20th of this October month. For some moments throughout the day, I wish I could be by her side—to comfort my sister in marriage, to murmur soothing words to her, to see to little John's meals and diapers, to ensure that her gracious heart is not endangered by her grief.

And yet, I am not ashamed of my own contentment.

CHAPTER 3

CAMPS

Kaladouran, Syria - July 1915

LOUISA

Our village is unrecognizable today. Everyone is milling about the market stalls, faces flush with panic. Worse, not a soul is complaining about the heat bearing down; it is trapped in a smoldering haze that refuses to relent or allow even an instant of breeze to sneak down from the mountain; there is no hint of impending rescue from any quarter. We normally count on the mercy of the towering mountain in July but it appears to have abandoned us. Most residents push their way to the big fountain, intent upon gathering a glimmer of information before they rush back to the houses to prepare for what none of us yet understand. There are few men remaining who have not been taken to the army, and some of them are gathering in the village's two churches to discuss. What there is to discuss, however, is hard to guess. It is not as though there are alternatives to following the instructions that are posted.

The gendarme who tacked the paper on the stone pillars by the fountain walked away silently. Then another of them closed in to read it, and announced loudly that it said for us to be ready tomorrow. We must gather only what we can carry and leave—to where, no one knows. There have been rumors of towns emptied of their occupants, but none of the Kessab region have been forewarned. We do not even know if the town center in Kessab is in the same state of flux as we are. The rumors are unsettling but who can know the truth? The missionaries of Kaladouran are making rounds to houses to discuss matters. I overheard one of them say to another that we are lucky, that we will head south. What does that mean? Why is it lucky to head south? I was unable to ask in the chaos surrounding me.

At home now, I am contemplating how to sort our belongings, and trying to calm Mayrig, when Asadour's cousin knocks.

"Have you heard from him?" Shoushan, too, is concerned for my fiancé, Asadour.

"Not since April. Oh, Shoushan. He will not know how to find us!" I can no longer hold back the despair I have withheld for my mother's sake. "Giragos and Zarigh have received nothing either!" I know that Asadour's parents must be equally panicked. They cannot get word to him, any more than I can. I suddenly think of the letter, the last. I snatch the paper from my bureau drawer and hand it ceremoniously to Shoushan, willing her to read it and to discover some detail I may have missed that will shed new hope.

"Ah, Mary is now a bride in a new country. Who would ever have imagined?" She lifts her eyes and notices my tears.

"Louisa-jan, try to be grateful that Asadour is safe, away from here. And he will come." When she hands it back, I fold and stuff the paper into my skirt pocket.

We know there is war swirling about us. But I am suspicious and uneasy about this development. What will happen to our houses? Our livestock? Gardens? Some of the donkeys are allowed to go with us, to carry some of our things, but we must walk the entire way. Father and Mother are old for such walking and my little brother is too small. At least I can carry him. Mary, my younger sister, can walk herself, at least for a time. We do not know what is happening to relatives in the other villages or in town. My students at the school. I usually smile at the thought of them already seated in the classroom when I arrive each morning from my walk to Kessab proper, but today, I imagine them trying to make sense of this confusion and fear stabs at me from yet newer directions.

In the morning, I waken with the same deadening fear that has pervaded my sleep and refused me a moment of respite. Our household is desperately quiet; focused on what items to carry, we tread between rooms and make last minute choices. Hayrig has buried some metalware in the back yard and also packed a few silver plates for financial back up. The bag that falls against my back is stuffed with extra shawls; though warm now, we do not know when we will return. We are to report to the fountain in the center of the village, all twelve hundred or so residents of Kaladouran. Those with donkeys hang back at the edges of the group, to avoid the rebellious kick of an animal that can panic among the general sweat and fear oozing from such a crowd, not to mention the emotional tension. The buzz of voices has become a tone that is not normal and the din traps thoughts in my head, which I shake to clear.

I am comforted to see Shoushan and Shamo Titizian among the villagers winding up the gorge toward the fountain, their three older daughters holding the hands of younger Nazalee, Hovanes, and two-year-old Josef. Even while gently rubbing her swollen belly, Shoushan is watching little Josef squirm in Frieda's grasp, probably calculating how soon she will be carrying him. I search for my future in-laws, Giragos and Zarigh (called Kitcha) Karamardian. The children should be easy to spot; the twins are my age and Stepan is especially tall. Gulenia is already seventeen and even Manas and Khatches are tall enough to stand out. Where can they be?

Ah, there! On the perimeter. Asadour's sisters are slipping in and out of sight while moving through the crowd. They are such beautiful girls, especially my dearest friend, Louisa. I allow myself an instant to envision them all clad in identical wedding frocks on the day that I will marry their brother. Then I raise my arm and try to gain their attention. But it is only for that brief moment that I think I have seen Mariam and Gulenia at the outskirts of the group, then I lose them. I wonder if I really saw them at all. I look around at the large group and it occurs to me how very few men there are. Only the eldest of men are in our group; gathered here are mostly women and children, the majority of us representing the eldest and youngest of our village.

There will be no protection from within our group, so I pray hard that the gendarmes are merciful. The Missionaries who have come to see us off are still moving through the crowd to speak the words of comfort and assurance that we received when several came to the house. I notice Miss May reaching up to speak with a guard astride his saddle, and so I have cause for hope. She reaches our family and speaks with an intended calm that I, as a teacher, recognize as necessary to discourage fearful reactions.

"You people of Kaladouran are the first group to evacuate. Kessab townspeople will be sent in one month's time. The government officials have assured me of the safe passage of this group. Go with God." I tell myself to be comforted by her words. What else can we do?

As we pass by the farthest church, and then the last house in Kaladouran, it occurrs to me that my birthday will come next month, and I wonder where I will pass it. My fantasy of celebration with the glorious welcome home of Asadour has long faded. In his letter, he said that his plan to travel home this summer is now delayed. Due to war in Europe, there is no transport available for leisure passengers and all five of the Kessab men, having completed their studies, are stranded in Amirka for now. He says he will move on to Detroit, Michigan, and look for work near his cousins. The thought of them instantly sends my mind to Ladehkiya, to Marta and Nishan, the last of Bedros and Tzaghir Karamardian's children in this country. We learned from Asadour's letter that Mary was safely delivered to her brothers. Asadour himself accompanied her on a train. I allow myself a moment to fantasize that we are marching to Ladehkiya for safety, just as we had done to escape the Turkish attack on Kessab six years ago, and that we will reunite with our families there. But as the afternoon sun lengthens long past the half day's walk to the large city, I abandon such illusions. I still can spot none of Asadour's family on the trail, which worries me. The six gendarmes that accompany us ride about ten paces to one side and spread out along the long line of my villagers. I make a point not to look at them.

The first day we walk long past nightfall. No one is allowed to rest. My father fell once and was prodded up with the bayonet wielded by a gendarme from atop his horse. The guards stop at times to chew on food they carry. At least once I saw them take food away from some of our people attempting to nibble on what they had brought while stumbling along the narrow path. They do not allow us to stop for eating or drink. I try not to look back at my father and mother, lest they see the water in my eyes at the sight of their struggle, which I am sure is far beyond my own. Mary has been crying since the sun lowered over the horizon, and I have grown weary of responding to her with comforting tones. I grow silent.

We are not driven along the main roads that would have brought us right through Ladehkiya but are pushed through paths that lead inland, southeast. The dry summer sun is relentless, and the dusty trail offers no vegetation or shade. When at last the line of villagers is told to halt, the bodies all along it simply drop to the ground from where they stood, my father among them. Mother, too, slides downward in slow motion to slump beside him. The men on horseback ride back and forth up the lines but they do not call out and so we do not know how much time we will have to rest. I lower my brother to the dirt, and Mary and I lean against the three of them so that we form a hive of flesh clinging together and, before a single thought can invade and disrupt me, I fall asleep.

By the second day we are so used to being hungry that the cries coming from others up and down the trail line no longer intrude upon my inner numbness. This time, when we stop to rest in the darkness, I note that the line has fallen out of formation and is crumpled together. We are on a ridge and, when the march resumes and I step a few feet apart from our group, I can see for quite a distance behind me. Many people scattered along the trail have dropped in permanent exhaustion, no longer part of the moving line of villagers. When we next come to a longer halt, I seek out Shoushan but not enough light remains to illuminate faces, and we are all incognito, a human mass of suffering. I turn to look at my mayrig and hayrig and am overcome with fear that they may not endure the journey, whatever the destination. Dear God in Heaven, do not let it be so! May these thoughts flee from my sick and exhausted mind. Their faces betray nothing, and I know they are determined not to frighten the little ones. These thoughts are interrupted by a scream from the gathering dusk that pierces my consciousness. An animal? A girl? The dread is instant. I have heard about girls being dragged into the darkness and used and sometimes stabbed afterwards. Some girls take their own life after this. But I am not certain of what I heard and it has now ceased.

On the fifth day, Father again collapses. Mother lets out a shriek that climbs up my back and I twirl on my heels, heart pounding, desperate to reach him before the gendarme. By this time the gendarmes have been cruelly jabbing at the fallen with their bayonets, to keep the line moving. I have seen them spear right through the bellies of some of our people. By now we have learned not to stop, not to try to help our neighbor, not to yell our indignations… but to keep walking and concentrate on staying upright on the path, lest we lose our footing and perhaps our lives. When Hayrig falls, Mayrig and I try to pull him up, desperately begging him, pleading. With Garabet still on my hip, I try to help as best I can, grabbing under the opposite arm from the one Mayrig is yanking on, willing his lifeless body to react. This time there is no resisting the tears.

"Dear God Almighty, help us now. Please, please, Hayrig…" It is no use. Father has lost consciousness and stopping is not possible with the gendarme bearing down on us, bayonets poised above our heads. We stumble on, misery in every step. Mother and Mary sob for almost twelve hours, until the next sleep at darkness when they surrender to the exhaustion of tears coupled with more steps than should be humanly possible. I could not allow myself to cry. Not now.

Ironically, the very next day we arrive. At first, I'm not sure where. It is a city, and we are herded together in the outer end of town, pushed into an endless sea of people as ragged as we. Bread is passed out once a day. There is a trough of water, the kind I have seen used for horses and goats. We attack it, plunging our faces into the water just like everyone else.

Father missed bread by one day, I think. My tears come now, unashamed. More of our people arrive by the hour, and the camp swells with the sick and hungry. I have lost track of the people of Kaladouran; it is all I can do to keep close to Mother, Mary, and Garabet. Gratefully though, I run into Shoushan after a few days. She is pushing her way through the crowd in search of a doctor for the infant in her arms. I realize how the hot sun may have endangered the child cocooned in the sling on her back, unable to access her breasts while moving all day.

"No, Louisa, my baby is gone. I gave birth to his dead body and buried him under a mulberry tree on the fourth night of darkness." I want to touch her arm in sympathy, but Shoushan is almost twelve years older, and the gesture does not feel natural. She is a woman who comforts others and appears incapable of self-pity. Yet her eyes are pooled with the kind of sadness that neither language nor touch can heal.

"This baby is—was—Anahid's, my neighbor; she collapsed and… did not make it. I am nursing this one while I have milk, but I fear the child will need a miracle." Within minutes of her words, she is swallowed into the crowd and I lose sight of her.

I do not see Shoushan again. The next day, I learn from others that we are in Homs. But some of the crowd are being moved out on the road to Amman; I wonder if Shoushan and her family are among them. I cannot say that I prefer to go there; I do not imagine any of us can walk more. I do not know how long we will be where we are, how long we can live on bread, or how long the war will last. But at this moment I care not about any of these things. I just want to rest and, thanks be to God, sleep comes easily.

On a cold morning mid-way through winter, my mother does not awaken in our tent. I actually hear myself implore her she is not being fair to us! I am numb, empty, alone, and most of all, I am terrified to discover that I am not surprised. What can it mean that death no longer registers on a scale of astonishment? I cannot say how she died: lack of food, lack of medical care, a broken heart, any or none of these things is possible for a woman in her forties. A neighbor helps me bury her, though we make a helpless pair: two mud-caked women without a shovel, using hands and cooking utensils. Our world no longer includes strong men.

I know it seems strange, even surreal, that I have no time for mourning, but I am a girl of nineteen years and the head of my small family. I must figure out how to survive, to someday return home. It is not hard to move among the throngs of exhausted and starving people from Syria, some from the Cilician villages over the mountains from Kessab. I bargain for extra shawls and bread to keep my brother and sister warm and fed, pulling them along wherever I go. I have long since sold off what few possessions we managed to drag along on the march, including Hayrig's silver cups that somehow escaped the gendarmes' notice. I decide to fill up the endless hours, make myself useful, and eventually approach some volunteers. I have been watching these *odar* who appear, if not in charge of the camp, to have some sort of impact. They are always busy distributing food and blankets. They are foreigners, like the missionaries at home.

I tell them I am a teacher and immediately an arrangement is made: I am paid in food rations to run some outdoor classrooms, without books or study tools. Within days, children flock to the class. There is not room for all the students who ask, so we manage to rotate groups into learning schedules. I end up teaching large groups of children of all ages, in three different segments each day. It reminds me how precious learning is to Armenians, boys and girls alike. I must reach into the recesses of my own memories for lessons to teach my new students to

CHAPTER 4

NAMES

Kessab, Syria - August 1915

ALICE

Kessab is a big town, and when something special happens it comes alive. I can hear and see the excitement in the faces of all grown-ups. People move faster up the hills and down the streets and to the schools and churches. We have three churches in our town: Apostolic, Catholic, and Evangelical where the missionaries are. The churches give the most clues when important things happen. Everyone rushes there first for information. The sound of voices gets bigger, too; louder, in the churches and in the streets. At the market there is always lots of shouting and extra people join the shoppers, but Mayrig says it's to gossip, and we should carry on. Normally, I find out whatever is really important at my school, from the missionaries.

The thing that felt most amiss this summer was that we have not been to the family home at Kaladouran. I am eleven now and I hoped to see Marta there, to see that my prayers for her have been answered and perhaps she is not so sad. Also, all the people of town did not walk up the mountain to celebrate the Feast of Surp at Barlum Monastery like we have done every other August. Summertime is normally full of fun things, and we usually spend a lot of time at the beach and Uncle Giragos' gardens. But though it was as hot as every other August, we were at home, where I played with my cousins. Or, was I dreaming?

At first I was not alarmed at the commotion from the street outside. It seemed far away and unrelated. I had heard the uncles talking late last night, before I drifted to sleep, but it did not concern me. This morning Father and Mother joined Uncle Shamo at the schoolhouse in Kessab center for some speech or announcement or something. I thought maybe it was about school plans. Aunt Esther stayed home with us, and we were all in the garden to stay cool: me and Vartouhi and Vahan playing with Frieda, Anna, and Dikran. But when the shouts began to sound closer and moved fast up our street, my aunt called to me to look after the littler ones while she ran to the front of the house to see what was happening.

In a motion so fast the air swirled around her, she was back inside, screaming at us to gather close. She swooped up Dikran and leaned down close to my face, hissing intensely, "Elisa, your father is shot! Turks are coming to all the houses. I'll see to Shamo, then come back for you three. If they get here first—Elisa, this is important—be sure to tell them your father is in the army!"

And she was gone. Vartouhi clung to my skirt and I frantically looked for Vahan. I called to my mother but she was not in the house.

Pulling Vartouhi with me to the front steps, I called Mayrig's first name as loudly as I could. Screamed it, really. "Lulia! Lulia! Mayrig! Lulia! Lulia! Lulia!" We were both sobbing when three strange men bounded up the steps. I recognized their head garb, Turkish.

"Where are your parents?" The voice was gruff and scary. I remembered something…

"M-m-m-my father is in the army…" I stammered, still sobbing.

One of the men grabbed me by the elbow and began to pull us down the steps, Vartouhi still clinging to my skirt. A cart pulled by a horse was on the street and it pulled over when the man made a sign to its driver. I thought, they are going to take us away!

"M-m-m-m-m-my brother! Vahan!" I remembered, and yelled out his name. I hoped he would come running to us though I did not know what Turks do with little children. There have been many stories but, as in all monster stories, I did not really know what to believe.

Both men lunged forward. One grabbed Vartouhi away from me; the other raced up the steps and into the house. I imagined Vahan hiding inside, perhaps in a closet. I wanted to wish for something, but I didn't know what was better: that he remained hidden or that the man found him to join us. I did not know what to think about anything so again I screamed my mother's name. The next moment I was in the cart that wheeled me away from my home, away from Hayrig and Mayrig. Wheels creaked up and up the slopes of Mount Aqra, away from Kessab.

Tears spent, through the dark night I slept, hunched over my lap. At first light, I sat up and looked around, immediately aware that I was far from any familiar sights. I saw on the back of the cart maybe fifteen white-faced children blinking wide pools of fear from eyes both brown and grey. But no Vartouhi. No Vahan. A prickly tingle that began between my legs soon washed through me. No mother, no father. I looked at the turban on the head of the driver and felt the bile rise in my throat. I instantly needed to throw up and twisted my body to release last night's supper into the dim air behind the bench I was sitting on. The driver glanced back at me and laughed like a hyena. I know only some Turkish words, but I think his snarly comment was something like, "Looks like the wind will blow your dinner to the rest of them for breakfast!"

The cart took us to a very big city and straight to a big station with lots of tracks going in every way. I knew enough Arabic letters to read *Aleppo* at the top of the station. They put all of us on a train. In the train were hundreds and hundreds of children, mostly boys. But no mothers and fathers. A man came and passed out bread. A woman—I could not tell if she was a missionary or some sort of other lady saint with bushy black eyebrows under a head scarf— came by with ladles of something hot to drink. They both came twice that day. And the next. The train stopped many, many times, in every town it passed by. Each time it stopped, a group of boys was taken off the train. At every town between Aleppo and Constantinople, they put some boys, but no girls.

They brought us to a big building in the city of Constantinople. More Arabic letters above the big green doors spelled some name of an orphanage. This time I didn't recognize enough of the letters to read it. There were mostly boys there, I think five hundred or so, and only about thirty girls. The people told us to make a line inside an enormous room that looked like a church. Then a woman walked down the line and stopped in front of each boy and girl and wrote something down. When she did that, she said a name. Girls around me started to cry. After a little time I realized why. They were changing our names! I thought I may as well melt into the floor and disappear. I slid right down to that cold floor and like the girls around me, I wailed and wailed. I did not care if I would be beaten for it. I wailed for my mother and father and sister and brother, and I wailed some more for me. I could not hear my own voice amid the keening that seemed to echo around the walls and up to a ceiling so high I could not have seen it were I not laying on the tiles beneath that lady's feet. I was not the only one. Not one of us could stop the deafening sound from bursting from our souls. Not a child among us could bear to stop being ourselves, no matter what fate was in store for us.

After a while of weeping, two new women came to that big room. One of them had a cane to help her walk, and she wore a hat unlike any I'd ever seen. It was the same pink color of her dress and it was wide, with a netting that almost covered her face, but both of the ladies were dressed differently from the Muslim 'naming' lady. The other lady was tall and though she spoke in our language, she didn't look like one of us. Her blouse and skirt were clean and shiny and she held her head higher than our mothers and aunts did. Like angels, the ladies slowly walked up and down our line, shushing us and talking in low tones, over and over until everyone could hear their words over our howling. So in time, we slowed our cries to whimpering and sniffling, and listened.

"Don't worry, there are lots of Armenians in Constantinople. When the war is over, they will come and get you."

I did not know if we should believe these ladies, but I told myself then, that I would memorize my name and all the names I could think of from my family and never, ever forget them. In case I could be Armenian again and be myself. Eventually I stopped my whimpers; there was no use.

We had school to learn Turkish. Then we had school to learn other things.

For three years, I was called Fatima.

CHAPTER 5

CARTS

Latakia, Syria - September 1915

MARTA

Nishan's house was more than ten blocks from our home in Ladehkiya but still near the Armenian quarter. My brother forbid me to wander near our old house, said it was not safe for me to do so. I, now a young lady of fourteen, could no longer walk alone in the streets. He sternly explained that Turks steal wives at my age, that they have no shame or respect for females, particularly Armenian girls. Nishan's house was smaller than ours was, and much more crowded with the children. But the children were my salvation. Even when I thought of Hayrig, of Mary, even when my heart wanted to crack and I thought to throw myself down the well, I found my way back through the sound of the children saying my name. As I snapped back to present, I noticed they may be laughing in a game and waiting for me to approve some little child's joke that Zaha made. Ah, Zaha especially! How I love that child. Mary, too, of course. But Zaha and I have a special connection. The thought made me smile as I turned from the washing basin and surveyed the children sitting around the table laughing with my sister-in-law.

We had just finished our breakfast. The door burst open with no warning and people were shouting inside. I left the children's plates I was washing and raced from the kitchen to see what the sounds were. Four squat men, with conical fezes that gave them more height, were squeezed into the corridor, pushing Nishan against the wall!

He was saying something to them, over and again. "I have done nothing! What do you want?" But then one of them pulled out a long pistol and held it up to his head. I jumped at the bang! Nishan slid down the wall with so much blood streaking behind him on it.

He stopped, slumped there on the ground, lifeless. But there was no stillness. No time to understand. Lousine screaming, I heard her first and now I saw her. I was not screaming, not breathing. Could not breathe.

The Turkish gendarmes, brutes with funny hats, herded us into the eating area, the children clutching to Lousine and me, simpering in fear, but I was not there, not really: I had gone to a different place in my head, with Hayrig and Mary and all my family in a big garden at the house in Kaladouran, eating watermelons and pomegranates. And laughing! And…

Sharp, ugly voices interrupted my fantasy. I clung tightly to Zaha as we were pushed again, this time shoved out to the front of the house. There were two carts on the street, with more men behind the horses. One of the men began yelling and pointed to Lousine.

From my school work, I understood his Turkish words clearly. "I'll take that one for a wife!" Everyone knows that Turks have multiple wives and I felt Lousine shudder, even though I did not look at her directly. I was wildly looking about for the children.

"What about the Armenian dog brats?" another one laughed when he said it.

"What the hell. Free labor!" That man roughly jerked Lousine towards the second cart, which caused her almost to drop the baby.

Little Mary and the boy did not let go of her skirt and shuffled along with her, somehow. Zaha was still glued to my side, and we were both frozen. I tightened my grasp on her, unwilling to let go of the last of my family. Time stood still for a moment, or a year, I don't know. But when Zaha whimpered for her mother I instinctively came alive and hissed to her, "Run to Mayrig. Now!" Zaha stumbled to Lousine just as her mother was being pushed into the cart. But two hands grabbed the girl by her waist and held her back. Lousine and I held a collective breath, the helpless, desperate question suspended in the air. We looked from the man holding Zaha to the man on the driver bench. Finally the driver of the cart that held Lousine and the children gave a shrug. Zaha was flung onto the cart just as he whipped the horses and started off with a jolt that flung Lousine's head backward. The last sight of my family. Creaking wheels, clunk of horse hooves. The last sounds.

Nishan's body was still lying in the corridor inside, and I strained for time to think, to look over my shoulder toward where my brother lay. Instead, my blood went cold with new understanding. I was alone with the remaining men—and the wrong cart! My family disappeared in minutes. I was fourteen, too old to assume that all would be well, too young to know enough to avoid thinking about what might lay ahead. My mind was off on a journey of no return and no comfort as the slave camp cart rumbled away. With me.

And rude men who leered at me.

CHAPTER 6

WAR

Port Huron, Michigan - 1917

JOE

As far as Joe was concerned, the best thing in the whole state of Michigan was the little ten-acre farm he found to rent in Port Hune. True, he had moved his family around the state. Morton Salt Company provided plenty of work, but twice he returned to the Highland Park auto plants, the last time to help settle his sister, Mary. He even worked once at the salt plant in Flint, a town that neither he nor Helen had much use for. It galled him to pay rent when his new country offered plentiful land to buy, but the landlord would not sell and he had yet to find a setting as suitable as this farm. The tiny acreage in Port Hune (the way he and his family pronounced Port Huron) served his emotional needs, offering him the ability to divide his time between the baking ovens at the salt plant and the glory of sun and soil in his vegetable fields.

In short time, Joe cultivated a Spanish customer base in the surrounding hills, similar to the one he had serviced on the

Dominican island, and blessed God for his weekends of farm life. On Saturdays, he hitched up the cart and horse, loaded ripe tomatoes, fruits, and squash, and disappeared into an old fantasy of camaraderie. Speaking Spanish again was a pleasure and often the invitation to a game of dominoes stretched the day longer than intended.

Helen, too, was happiest here. She thrived in the flourishing Syrian community that included her brother's growing family and took special pride in hosting services at their home whenever the priest arrived in town to offer mass. On Sunday summer afternoons, they regularly entertained hundreds of first generation Syrians in the large spaces of field and garden beside the house, with a distant but clear and impressive view of Lake Huron. Joe kept plenty of extra planks and sawhorses in the barn to haul outside every week for makeshift tables. He loved that Helen was proud of their role and, though he seldom thought of it, he had made an unconscious decision to remain silent about his true identity. Who cares? he thought. Let them assume I am Syrian. He suspected, however, his Protestantism to be the greater evil.

Helen's brother Moses had followed them. First, to Detroit where he met his wife, Mary. It was no-brainer for Moses to continue on to Port Hune and Morton Salt Company, a world he had experience with. He settled in the less desirable worker housing near Gratiot Boulevard, by the Marysville plant, an easy walk to work at the salt block and they saw him as often as possible. His two boys arrived in the alternate years between and after Henna and Jake; Mary was already due with a third child. Though Helen was not close to her brother, she was content with his proximity and happy to be raising their children together. Joe had no opinion about Moses, but noted he was more serious and subdued as a family man, making a valid effort to provide. He watched his own boys enjoy the gift of cousins.

"Nothing but boys around here!" Helen would mutter as they whooped and scrambled around the house, but he caught amusement in her voice as she said it.

Although life in Amirka had, by now, dulled Mussa's disapproval of his sister's marriage to an Armenian, and a non-Orthodox at that, Joe would not go as far as to call him a friend. Nevertheless, he and Helen always included Moses and Mary in their gatherings, and Helen made a point to invite them to mass whenever the priest was there. While they seldom accepted, they might casually appear afterward for the Sunday picnic festivities that followed the service. When she huffed up and pointed it out, Joe only laughed at her annoyance.

"Expectations are wasted," he replied, "on any but your own charges."

The outside world, particularly the world butted up against the farthest edge of the Mediterranean, had faded to a blunted memory up until Mary's arrival. Then war erupted. It seemed the biggest war Joe had ever heard of. It's all anybody talked about. Who was entering this war, where was the front, when would Amirka enter; whether, in fact, she would enter. Even before Joe Peter gathered up his small family after Mary's wedding and hustled them onto a train back to Port Hune the shoe shop conversation revolved around the big war. The Armenians and Syrians in his world monitored events, paying close attention to moves by the Ottoman Empire, praying that the war was not impacting Kessab and Cilicia, nor the Syrian coast snaking southward to Beyruth.

Almost three years since the first rumblings, there no longer existed, in any public or private location, conversation that wasn't dominated by war news that streamed in daily. On Sundays, when the priest came to say mass, and after Helen and the Syrians of Port Huron were full of prayer, the Arabic conversation that filled Joe's living room was of nothing else. On Saturdays, when Joe drove his cart full of produce to the Spanish-speaking neighborhood in the hills, his customers relied on him as much for news as for tomatoes and peaches. This pressure was challenging since he was dependent on others for the information; he could not read English. Sometimes Joe was grateful for the obsession with war that took his thoughts from the lingering grief for his father that had first appeared with the arrival of Mary, and then clobbered him inside his own home.

It was the morning of October 20, 1914, now two harvests and three winters behind them, but Helen's screams still stalked his sleep some nights. "Jirgis! Jirgis! Allah! Jirgis! Allah, In chah Allah!" He still ached for his second born. But he suffered even more the haunting memory of his wife's loving reach for tiny George, the gasp that quickly exhaled into a piercing howl, the panic frozen in time. How she patted, then pounded George on the back, desperate to force him awake, rocking the body in her arms, wailing, pleading to God Almighty. Joe had stood helplessly by, aware of little Henna across the room, who had heroically pulled himself up in the little bed pushed against the wall. Though he would never forget the loss of any young soul, Joe wondered almost immediately if time might heal. And how long? He was grateful to be more and more distracted by the great delight he took in his growing family.

Besides Henna (Johnny), now four, the family's loss of Jirgis (George) had been softened with two more arrivals: handsome Jacob was now two; and charming little Zaha (Laura), Helen's joy and crowning glory was, at seven months olds, already crawling and giggling and dominating the family's attention with her beauty. Although he himself was sincerely smitten with the child, his wife's relief at having a girl surprised him. It hadn't occurred to him how important it may be to running a large household; he assumed a stable of boys was the most important thing to ultimately keep up a farm and ensure family income. But this little goddess was a sight to behold and a force to be reckoned with. Joe's eyes were drawn to her nearly every moment he was in the house. When she began to say a few chosen words, like "Yalla, Henna!" as her tiny legs toddled through a room, her pudgy hands clutching at her big brother, or "shookran" (thank you) to Helen bending down to place a drink in her two hands, Joe's throat caught a swallow of air too fast and he imagined the swelling in his chest might strike him down before his breath could return to a steady rasp.

March brought the best surprise when Asadour once more walked up the long drive to the house and stayed on for a few weeks to help Joe with the spring planting. When war broke out across the ocean, almost two years ago now, and he discovered that returning to Syria was not immediately possible, Asadour found work in Indianapolis through a connection with a school companion. Joe wondered why he left the job but waited for his cousin to bring up the subject. Having him around was a treat and a big help. It was remarkably easy to hitch the horse and work the plow alongside Asadour, and both men were triggered with thoughts of Kaladouran and the garden shared by their fathers, in which they had been raised. They chatted amicably while in the field and on the pillared porch that wrapped the house on two sides; from there they could glimpse the lake, the same big lake sea from which they had watched fireworks in Detroit when Asadour had stopped for the holiday on his way to Indiana. It took Asadour a week to blurt out the thoughts he had carried to Port Huron to share with his cousin.

"Hovsep, I have written five times now. I heard nothing. Not from Hayrig, from Louisa, from Uncle Shamo, or Uncle Garabet. I tried them all. I fear the worst!" The cousins sat up all that night, speaking softly on the porch so as not to disturb Helen or the sleeping children.

"It must be the war. It is not possible for the post or telegrams to get through."

"The last telegram I got was to say that Mary was rescued and boarded in Beyruth. That was three years ago! But Hayrig also said then that Armenians are being conscripted into the army. Why did he say that? Armenians are supposed to be disqualified from serving in the Ottoman military!"

"That is what always happens in war. Those in power throw their minorities to the front of their own bodies. Don't you think so?"

Asadour sighed. "Still, no word since then. It's been three years!"

Joe swallowed his own thoughts; no word of Marta or Nishan had reached him or his brothers. But he feared losing his mind if he succumbed to what he could not know. It was clear to him that if he could plant himself firmly on the ground that supported him physically until such time as information appeared to act upon, he could survive almost anything. But this was easy for him, easier than for Asadour who had everything to lose back home. He glanced sympathetically at his cousin. "What is your plan?"

"Detroit. I feel certain that the United States will enter this war and I am thinking maybe there is a way to get home."

"How? And why leave your job for Detroit?" Joe was patient but confused.

"Cousin Boghos wrote me from New York. You remember Aunt Mary's boy, the reason I came to Rochester to study? The Americans call him Paul, the Armenians nicknamed him Ingeles because he speaks good English. When we got stuck here he went to the big city for work. New York. But Boghos heard of Armenians who are fighting with the French in the Levant against the Turks! In Cilicia, at home, Hovsep! I must make contact with those persons who are recruiting the Armenians here. So many Armenians in Detroit, isn't there bound to be a recruiter, a connection?"

"For the French army? This does not make sense."

"La Legion d'Orient. They have taken in one thousand Armenian soldiers already from France and Amirka. They are called Gamavor because we volunteer. When we enter the war, I can find my way."

"What makes you sure that Amirka will fight? Wilson says no, stay neutral."

"Hovsep, where have you been? The government just passed a new law for the money! U.S. Congress. They gave the money for war, so that means it is happening. Any day now."

"I wish the best for you, Asadour. But be careful what you wish for. I would not go near a goddamn Turk again for all the money in Amirka."

"Hah! There is no avoiding Turks back home. But Hovsep, I must get home!" Asadour's cry turned from sullen to desperate.

After this, Joe made it a point to keep up with the flowing news however he could, loitering in shoe shops and barber shops, eavesdropping on street conversations. Best of all, Asadour could read English with his fancy education so two or three times a week, they bought a daily newspaper, which Asadour read aloud to him. Four more U.S. merchant ships were sunk by U-boats and the clock stopped ticking. Sure enough, true to Asadour's belief, on the second day of April:

"President Woodrow Wilson went before Congress and called for the declaration of war against Germany! Hovsep, it has happened," he yelled.

On the third of April, Joe accompanied his cousin to the train and embraced him. "I figure I'll see you by autumn, cousin." He planned to move the family back to Highland Park and, for the following winter, take advantage of increased hours and pay that Ford Motor Company was advertising. Joe assumed that, with men enlisting in war right and left, positions would be plentiful. But he would first have to harvest the gardens and lend the cow to a neighbor grateful for the milk. He, of course, would have no part of war. His family, his life, was rooted.

On June 5, 1917, a trio of Karamardian men—Archie (as Khatchig was now called), Leo, and Asadour—descended the stoop of 98 Kendall Avenue in Highland Park and walked to the brick recruitment office together. There they chatted with neighbors and Ford employees while waiting in the long line that circled the block, a line dominated by Armenians, Syrians, and Greeks. Some Polish and other immigrant groups were also among the residents of apartment blocks such as those on Cottage Grove (mostly Armenians), Victor Ave (Syrians), and Woodward, where Leo's shoe parlor was located and where he and Archie worked together. All three men registered as single and unburdened by wives or dependent siblings, though Leo's artificial leg was duly noted and undoubtedly exempted his call to duty. (The Simon brothers, all living at 130 Victor Avenue with their wives and parents, would not register until the following year on September 10, 1918.)

The man at the recruitment office knew nothing of foreign legions, nor did he seem to care. But Asadour returned once a week until July, when the man agreed to make an inquiry. The last day he walked into the office, the man looked up at him with a frown.

"It seems there is no recruitment for what you want. We are not at war with the Ottoman government."

Asadour trudged silently back to Kendall Avenue thinking, this cannot be the end of it. But less than one hour later, his frustration dissolved instantly when he discovered that a wire from cousin Boghos, in New York, awaited him at the house.

"Leaving tomorrow for training with French Foreign Legion. Stop. Paterson, NJ. Stop. Come." The Karamardian cousins tried to dissuade him. Leo thought him mad, but Archie was more rational and offered his advice.

"Look, if you remain in the U.S. you have a far better chance of sending for Louisa after the war and successfully acquiring her entry papers."

"Khatchig, that is not the point. There is only silence from Kessab. I cannot find any of them if I do not go. I promise to write when I learn of your sister and brother as well." He could not blame his cousins for not sharing his sentiment. Their lives were established in the U.S. and there were no chosen ones to return to. Besides, any military future for the physically impaired Leo was out of the question. Nonetheless, Archie Karamardian, in a burst of patriotism for his adopted country, decided to enlist with the Americans.

CHAPTER 7

LEGIONNAIRES

Oceans and Continents - 1917

ASADOUR OF GIRAGOS

On the train that steamed east across the endless green landscape of Ohio and Pennsylvania, Asadour considered the monotonous sound of the metal spokes clanking beneath his feet. They seemed to make a mockery of his anxiety. He felt as if he were on a planet far from anything resembling his home, too far away to make his way home. The rhythm of metal striking against railroad track spurted out names of his siblings: Gu-le-ni-yah, Ste-pan, Ma-ri-am, Khat-ches, Kit-cha, Ma-nas, Gi-ra-gos, Gi-ra-gos, Gi-ra-gos….and Lu-i-sa. His father's name became stuck inside the rhythm and repeated endlessly. The journey across green, flat and sometimes hilly landscapes to New Jersey felt endless, but seemed only a fraction of his imminent future.

He realized, with some foreboding, that the journey to Kessab would be long, with many detours, any one of which may cost him his life. He glanced around the car packed with men whose faces seemed to match his own resolve and thought how the solidarity of patriotism was a wondrous thing. Only his patriotism was not exactly what these others might expect, as they hurtled to join their American regiments, so he kept his plans to himself. When anybody asked him his military division or regiment he replied simply.

"Paterson, New Jersey. Training."

By July, he was on the ship *L'Espagne*, speeding to Bordeaux with 1,200 other men who had completed initial training in New Jersey. Bunked with Boghos, the two compared tidbits of information, trying to piece together their immediate future. The ship's speed was unusually fast, in part to evade U-boats lurking the seas. It had been seven years since Asadour and Boghos, together with the Churukian brothers, sailed across the Atlantic Ocean toward North America to begin studies. Now retracing those steps, in only a matter of weeks he may cross the Mediterranean back to Syria's shore—to family and Louisa.

"My last letter from home came in May, 1915. They posted it in February." Boghos was as concerned as everyone else on the ship, none of whom had heard from family in at least two years. They met hundreds of colleagues from Kessab on the ship and at the French military medical center in Bordeaux, including his old chum Vahan Churukian. But reconnecting with school chums from childhood was bittersweet since Asadour received glum news from these men. News from Kessab was not specific, but it could be assumed to be as desperate as the general accounts trickling in of deportations and atrocities.

Back in New Jersey, the recruiter Damadian had made the mission clear and convincing. Asadour's fear for his family had opened a gaping space in his heart that welcomed the message and filled him with purpose. It was promised that Gamavor were to fight only the Turks and only in Cilicia. Post war, they would form the backbone for a new Armenian army of a new Armenian Republic that would bring freedom and self-rule to the many Armenian villages of Cilicia. This promise was worth the detour of any battle preceding a victorious return home.

"Imagine, Ingeles! A Cilicia for Armenians," he murmured often to Boghos.

Realistically, Asadour knew he was powerless over the immediate future, even vaguely understood that helplessness around the fate of his people was more than any man should have to bear. Every man around him felt the same; there was nothing to do but rush forward and face the oppressor. Still, he held out hope that the innovative Kessab people had managed some brilliant, or even miraculous, survival. His father, Giragos, possessed practical leadership skills among the villagers of Kaladouran; surely, he had discovered some solutions. Unrealistically, he thought his people blessed, deserving of any miracle that God may grant.

All the men on the ship carried an important piece of paper, an official document from the U.S. declaring honest intent to serve in the Legion, signed by Mehran Sevalsky, and necessary for admittance to the French army; Asadour fingered his as he waited to disembark at port. The authorization handed over, Asadour and Boghos (called 'Ingeles,' by most of the Legionnaires) entered the medical center for testing of physical aptitude for military combat. Asadour found the testing to be nothing out of the ordinary and far less strenuous than basic training. He also learned that the Armenians from the United

States were valued for their facility with the English language and wondered why the French concerned themselves with this. A French navy ship then transported the group across the Mediterranean to Cyprus, where the military training was to become intense and specific.

For ten months they formed platoons and battalions, studied military war and science, and practiced intensive exercises of war. Asadour learned to shoot weapons, including artillery guns, and was introduced to (and reacquainted with) even more townspeople from Kessab who had preceded him to the La Legion d'Orient, such as Ovsia Saghdejian and Misak Giragossian. But the men who inspired him most were the Djebelis of Musa Dagh.

He and the Kessab men were assigned to the lower part of camp Monarka, a section called Camp Souedie that had been built by men from Musa Dagh. Kessab and Musa Dagh were neighboring towns on either side of a pair of mountains. As one of the Djebeli men exclaimed, "Look east over the water. There is our home, right there, beyond our eyes! We are so close, yet so far from family…"

These men confirmed to Asadour that Kessab, like Armenian communities everywhere in Cilicia and Turkey, had received orders of deportation and the Armenians were long removed. That explained the silence from family members. More importantly, it deepened the mystery as to their whereabouts. He also learned from the Djebelis of the forty-day siege on their Musa Dagh and that they had not gone along with deportation orders. Instead, most of their townspeople had accumulated weapons, climbed the mountain, and fought back when Turkish garrisons arrived to flush them out. The situation had been dire, turned even more deadly and surely headed to defeat and massacre had not the French warship *Guichen* appeared like a vision on the shoreline to rescue the surviving four thousand residents and transport them to Port Said. The Legion had originally been formed with five hundred of these brave men as its core, recruited at Port Said, seasoned fighters desperate to take on the Turks and enact their revenge. Asadour and Boghos, were awestruck in the presence of heroes.

"We sent a letter to the Kessab people and asked them to join us on the mountain," said Satrag, catching Asadour by surprise. He exchanged a look of wonder with Boghos.

"The Tashnag party decided we would not go," explained Hagop Apelian, a Kessabtsi.

"Always, the politicians decide for us! And not always correctly," added Nishan Chalabian. Asadour suspected that both of these men from Kessab would have gladly joined the men from Musa Dagh. He wondered about their escape and appearance on Cyprus and wished the conversation had continued, but the men were interrupted by an officer calling the regiment back to training.

When the troops were battle ready, they were transported by steam vessel from the island of Cyprus to Port Said. His first time on Egyptian soil, Asadour was not prepared for the sight of the refugee camp there. The squalor, the condition of thousands of his people, starving, ragged, haggard, hardly recognizable Armenians. At least three thousand of these ghost figures were women and children from the siege at Musa Dagh, having survived one nightmare only to be enduring a second. Asadour could not have recognized a few of his own cousins, clinging to the metal fence around the very dusty plazas he marched through. Fighting his own tears, he willed his thoughts to the coming deployment: focus on the Gamavor mission would surely protect from the despair now threatening to drown him.

By mid-morning the following day, the heat was not fit for human endurance, when all Legion troops were called together at Port Said and presented with their future. The dust that rose from hundreds of boots still swirled around the French commander of the Armenians, General Romieu, as he introduced to the men the top leaders of the French and British armies, along with the Armenian Junior Officer staff. A hush fell over the group as two men stepped forward.

The High Commissioner of Cyprus introduced the most important man in charge of the eastern theater: General Allenby of the British forces. He would be leading the forthcoming campaign into Palestine in an attempt to rout the Ottomans all the way from Palestine, Syria, and Cilicia. Allenby effectively laid out the Legion's mission. Asadour was glad he had enough grasp of the English language to comprehend the details, but grew more uneasy the longer Allenby spoke. Something was wrong.

As Allenby continued to describe the strategy for the Sinai Palestine Campaign, the Djebelis and Kessabtsis became visibly angry, Asadour and Boghos among them. The promise had been that Armenians would fight only in Cilicia, but they were now being routed to Palestine with the British Fifty-Fourth Infantry Division, which included two battalions of Arabs! Feet shuffled and voices among their group interrupted the English general, who paused, astonished at the outburst.

"This is not what we signed up for!" Misak was oblivious to the breaking of protocol with his outburst.

And Hagop picked it up, "We don't fight for broken promise!" The turmoil their words provoked among the Armenians was not to be controlled and so, with Romieu's entreaty, the troops were temporarily dismissed.

Betrayal is a hard emotion to overcome and required several more weeks of continual diplomacy from French and British alike toward the Armenian battalions. Meanwhile, Asadour felt his life sink like quicksand.

Boghos plainly verbalized the conundrum. "On the one hand, we are recruited to fight in Cilicia. With the other hand, we are sent to Palestine and made to fight our way to Cilicia!"

"Yes, but no matter the hand, how do we reach Kessab at all, if we refuse? Do we rot in Port Said while our families suffer the marches? What good are we to them here?"

Ultimately, the convincing came from two of their own: Officers Chankalian and Shishmanian, each having had experience with the U.S. Army and used to the inevitable compromises of ever-changing military policy, were also tuned into the pulse of fellow Armenians hungry for revenge. Neither man was particularly tall and both sported a style of moustache that suggested wealth, if not European education, of the time. But seeing a fellow Armenian of some level of authority in an army cap, rather than a fez, on this side of the ocean was rather encouraging to the cousins from Kessab. Shishmanian had a command in his voice that invoked pride in the infantry subjects before him and his eyes mesmerized the men. Asadour thought he could follow this man into a sea of bullets without hesitation. The officer leaned down to the dirt, dragged over a block of wood about to be split for cooking fires, jumped on it and balanced himself for a moment. When satisfied that he was visible to each man in the platoon, he raised his voice but kept it even and steady.

"Think, men! This is the major endeavor in our homeland and brings together the full force of two major countries, plus anti-Turk Arabs, who are fierce allies. But in order for us to make it to Cilicia, the way must be cleared. The Yildirim Army Group of the Ottoman Empire is stationed in Palestine, supported by Germans. We will push the evil Turks north, away from our towns and our families. We will rescue many of our people on the way. We will earn our independence from the Turks with this—our Armenian contribution to squashing the Ottoman Empire—and reclaim Cilicia for Armenians. Are you with me?" A roar went up from the men.

Asadour resigned himself to what was considered by most of the Gamavor a detour from their intended mission. Since the British and French had merged for this major effort, he and his fellow soldiers would be handed over to Allenby's command of the operation; the French Armenian Legion (XXI Corps) was to be part of the Detachement Francais de Palestine et de Syrie. Asadour and Boghos were with their battalion when it shipped out from the Sinai, hugging the coastline, and came ashore in Jaffa. They came armed with military issued weapons and a renewed promise. They would march against the Yildirim Army and then be transported to Cilicia. It was now mid-September.

The march to Jerusalem took a day. After initial rest and organizing of supplies, Boghos and Asadour discovered they would have one day off duty with which to wander the streets of the fabled city from their school teachings of Jesus. But this was a city occupied by a western army comingled with Arab, Indian, Egyptian, and even Australian soldiers; there was little to be seen behind the dust, uniformed bodies, and autos and carts full of weapons.

Before dawn on the third day, the attack was launched and the XXI Corps was to head north toward the Turkish lines. Asadour awoke with the men of his regiment and silently hoisted his gear. They joined the full corps to march in silence. Southwest of Rafat, they stopped and rested with the darkness until three in the morning. The Armenian group then continued north and, within an hour, stopped to kneel and load. The command, barely visible in the quiet night, prompted Asadour and the others to open fire on the enemy at a location called Three Bushes. Loading and shooting was all he allowed in his head for the few hours endured in kneeling position. Before the first light, all resistance had ceased. His regiment advanced to the now silent Turkish trenches. With each step, Asadour sensed an unfamiliar dread descend upon him. His steps slowed until his foot finally felt the edge of a ditch.

He looked down at several living faces and smelled fear behind black eyes. For one wavering moment he was a soul suspended in time, floating above all humankind without motive or judgement, close to his savior and held by all the angels of all the worlds. But he then looked again into eyes, eyes that may have devoured one of his sisters or killed one of his aunts for no reason other than to exert personal power. The fear hovering behind at least one pair of eyes held knowledge of unspeakable sins against his family, his people. Without realizing that he was no longer frozen, he lifted his rifle, aimed towards a spot between those eyes, the spot where the brows met above the nose, and pulled the trigger. He looked around for Boghos, and spotted him farther down the trench line. What did he hope to see? With a bit of relief, he noticed the smoke settling from his cousin's rifle. But Boghos' face was not at peace. It seemed to match the sickness Asadour felt in his own stomach.

Within thirty minutes more they overtook Scurry Hills. This time Asadour did not trust his soul, his heart. He cursed the situation, feeling unworthy of the power presented to him. He managed to restrain himself from instinctively murdering his helpless enemies, vaguely aware that the group consciousness had reached the same decision. Securing the prisoners to a crop of mulberry trees for collection by the Brits advancing from behind, the Gamavor continued to Deir el Qassis and occupied it quickly. But almost immediately bullets whistled above Asadour's head, some landing close beside him; they were receiving fire from another direction: from a ridge they could not reach. Just as the command to abandon the area came, Asadour felt, more than saw, Boghos fall at his side. He dropped to his knees to inspect the wounds of his cousin. Although the blood was flowing, it appeared to be coming from one arm with multiple punctures. Asadour ripped his dust bandana and wrapped the arm, then helped Boghos to his feet to stumble down the slope with the retreating regiment. Once safely out of fire shot, he handed him off to a medic.

Only halfway through the mission, the XXI continued east to the highest point of battle, known as Arara. The Seventh

Ottoman army, from where they were entrenched in the heights above, bombarded mercilessly. Asadour's regiment pushed forward with a sort of collective consensus that there was nothing to lose and therefore nothing to fear. If the Turks were to escape and win, there was no future for themselves or their families. Through the night, with bullets invisible to the eye but audibly whizzing about their ears, Asadour and his compatriots climbed and crawled and fired—and fired—until targets ceased to present themselves to fire at. His limbs frozen with fatigue, Asadour could not imagine his body free of the aching it now was drowned in. But the goal was achieved.

It was first light of September 20th. When the sun rose over the ridge they had managed to take, the soldiers could see down onto the plains below and were stunned. Asadour memorized the scene before him: The Fifty-Fourth was fanning out in all directions, pivoting north, east, and west. He did not yet understand that this was because his own group of Armenians on the right flank had cleared the way for the entire military operation now advancing. The 163rd, the 164th, and there—racing up the center—was the horse brigade, arms clutching British flags and heads topped with turbans all galloped together! Asadour had never seen a war movie. The scene before him was more astonishing than any cinematic film that would be created in future decades to glorify the Great war, films that would hum and flash in American movie houses. Asadour would not see these, but he sucked in air and memorized the historic panorama unfolding below him.

CHAPTER 8

CILICIA

The Levant - 1918

ASADOUR OF GIRAGOS

Palestine had fallen to the Allies in one day. Some of the British brigades marched on to Damascus, some to Homs and Hama. Fortunately, Asadour and Boghos were unaware of that fact, and spared the agony of knowing they were being kept from reaching Syria. The Armenian fighters gathered their twenty-three dead and buried them on the ridge at Arara. Asadour and the Armenians were then marched towards Beyruth, a difficult trek, with the scarcity of food along the way adding to their misery. The march through Palestine and into the Lebanon was marked with wonder, grief, and utter despair.

At first, the many Christian ruins they passed raised the Armenian spirits with hope as they continued in the direction of their hometowns and villages. This was as short lived as the body of the first bone that crunched under a boot. With an abrupt halt and further inspection, the prickle born in Asadour's spine traveled further up, fanning outward at the wings of his back and on to his neck. Bones were strewn along the clogged roads, evidence of vulnerable Armenians who had succumbed to the death marches. Like Boghos and the other soldiers, Asadour descended rapidly into bitterness and rage. Almost worse, a few hours later the men encountered an elder Turkish man accompanied by two young girls seated in the back of the cart who, by their loose hair and vacant eyes, were easily identifiable as Armenian. The girls appeared too frightened to admit their heritage and didn't respond to the greeting lobbed at them in their own language as their Turkish elder drove on.

Near Haifa, the Armenian soldiers in their ragged French uniforms again approached a slow moving cart with an odd couple. This time they chose to confront and, even on foot, easily surrounded the pair, causing the old Turkish man to pull up tight on the reigns. His lips curled even tighter as he sat immobile and awaited their first move. Blatantly ignoring the man, Hagop Apelian spoke directly to the girl in Armenian.

"If you come with us, you will be safe. We will bring you to your family."

With hands clutching each end of her dusty head scarf, the girl kept her grey eyes trained on a spot in the distance and shook her head so imperceptibly that Asadour almost missed it, though he was within two feet of her. She declined to look at the men, or to be rescued, and the men reluctantly began to move on. At first, Asadour froze, disbelief threatening to swamp him, appalled at leaving her to her fate. When he finally stepped back into pace with the group, he felt a current of tension mixed with utter bewilderment among them. They marched in silence. After thirty minutes he worked it out.

And wept freely, unconcerned for the glances from some of his regiment. No doubt, these girls had already seen their families brutally murdered and had no future beyond the lives they now led. He prayed and prayed his sisters had not suffered this fate, nor, oh, God, please, his beloved Louisa.

After just one stop to rest, at Haifa, it was a relief to finally arrive at Beyruth where a new headquarters was established. The barracks were in a hotel whose owner, at first, refused to house the Armenians, until a French officer intervened. Such obstacles continued in every aspect of the Beyruth occupation. The Armenians were treated with disdain and disrespect by the mostly Muslim community of the city. In the streets, they were spat on.

One turbaned and bearded man callously barked at Asadour and Boghos, "If not for you dogs, my family would not have been driven from our lands by vengeful Turks! You do not deserve our hospitality!"

Once out of earshot, Boghos leaned over and growled to him, "Now we know we are home, cousin! Worse than *odars*, even, we are always dogs here!"

Like all tired Legionnaire soldiers who felt they had just fought someone else's battle, and were only too anxious to engage their own battle in Cilicia, the cousins were losing tempers and ready to defend themselves. The chaos intensified and did not appear to have a solution until command decided it best to remove the Armenians to the coastal city of Junieh, where they would await transport to Cilicia.

Here the name La Legion d'Orient was officially revised to La Legion Armenienne. (Evidently a decision had been made not to establish this name previously, in order to protect the Armenian population in Syria while under Ottoman control and at the mercy of Turkish wrath.) Once the Armistice was signed, the orders were given and the first three battalions were shipped to Mersina. Asadour and Boghos were gratefully transported with the Fourth Battalion to Iskenderun (Alexandretta), the closest point to, and north of, Kessab. Finally!

But it was clear from the moment they landed in the city that promises were to be broken again. Boghos and Asadour witnessed many a transaction on the streets and in the cafés, transactions they had grown up hearing about while under Ottoman rule. The French officers in the city were corrupt and prone to bribes. Disheartened and disgusted, they watched Ottoman officials lead young women to the French officers. It also was evident that some of the Arab troops that preceded the Gamavor to Iskenderun had already whipped up resentment toward the Armenians. The two cousins knew what it meant when they overheard two French officers discuss that the fault of some ruckus was to be placed on the Armenians, so as not to lose favor with the locals. In light of the corruption they saw, they feared and suspected that the promise and dream of an Armenian Army or Republic in Cilicia was an idealistic notion, highly unlikely to come to fruition.

"We should leave. Tonight," Boghos said it simply.

"Abandon our post?" Asadour felt skittish, a bit skeptical about the implications.

"Cousin, I feel quite certain no good will come of this scene. Not for us. Not for the Gamavor. It is done. Let's get home and do what we can for our own families. For Kessab!"

Asadour paused, fearful of what it meant to abandon the military he had fought with so intensely, with so much hope. What would it mean to surrender the purpose of all they had endured? What were they to strive for?

But he now said, simply, "I suspect you may be right, Ingeles," fondly using the nickname the soldiers had bestowed upon Boghos. At his core, he knew their cause was lost, and sighed. "Will there be no Armenian Army, then?"

"Only Armenian *Odars*, Asadour. As before and ever after."

Trudging through the mountain terrain proved to be more of a challenge than merely a physical difficulty. Marauding bands of Turks and Kurds were everywhere and the two men dared not sleep at the same time. They also came upon small groups of young Armenians, dragging their tired bodies along mountain paths on blistered and swollen feet, attempting a return home to villages that may no longer exist or, if they did, may not welcome them. The cousins tried to comfort these countrymen, who had lost most of their families and probably, all of their elders. At times they were able to point the poor souls in the best direction to avoid bandits whose whereabouts they had made note of. Finding food for themselves proved equally challenging. When they arrived at Musa Dagh, the hungry men stopped and rested, respectfully taking in the ruins of the village that had been bombarded by vengeful Turks. They gratefully hunted some of the wildlife that had grown emboldened and dared to draw close to the abandoned residences. Asadour hoped his Djebeli compatriots, now stationed in Adana and Mersina, would soon be reunited here to rebuild this honorable town.

Rested and with full bellies, Asadour and Ingeles walked half a day over Mount Aqra and came to the ruins of the Barlum Monastery. They kneeled in prayer. Until the summer of 1911, when they embarked for the United States, the two cousins had trekked to this monastery every August along with the entire population of Kessab, to celebrate the Feast of the Virgin Mary (Surp Asdvadzadzin, in Kessabsi). As they had when they were younger, they stood at the summit of the mountain and looked west, gazing at the Mediterranean glistening beyond. Then they looked to the east. They beheld a vision that was rare, visible only in certain conditions of light and weather, a mirage that had been seen and talked about by their parents: some claimed it to be the silhouette of Aleppo that was blinking from beneath clouds parting in the distance; others believed it the ruins of a castle atop a far off peak. Finally, they turned their faces south to behold their beloved Kessab. Asadour caught his breath. He exchanged a look with his cousin that meant more than words.

He'd followed his cousin to Amirka, then to war, and now back to Kessab. When Boghos was offered an opportunity to study in New York by his father's employer, Asadour had stumbled into a pot of luck no man had a right to dream of. It was decided by their fathers, Garabet (Boghossian) and Giragos (Karamardian) and some others that a group of young men be assembled for the journey and education, including his friends, the Churukian brothers. Even cousin Manas had joined in the convenience of the travel arrangements. When Asadour kissed his beloved Louisa goodbye, he had believed with all his heart the promise he whispered to her: "We will marry when I return. In three years' time." He now gazed down the mountain and swallowed. Seven years had passed. Would he find her? His thoughts embraced fantasies of his parents and siblings, how joyously they might reunite. But he dared not indulge long on these; since the trek through the Levant, he knew that hope could be a dangerous emotion.

They lingered a moment or two more before beginning the descent to town. The winter was milder than usual, but still challenging for any of the few survivors who gradually stumbled into Kessab, destitute of anything but threadbare clothing, yet clinging to life. Asadour and Boghos scoured the town for recognizable faces among survivors. Finding none, they walked on to Kaladouran. The village was empty and silent. They absorbed the silence and entered the gardens that adjoined Asadour's family home with the one Uncle Bedros had sold to the Merserlians when Asadour was just a small child. There was no sign of life. The overgrown garden was a tangle of brambles though some of the summer fruits had lingered. Asadour plucked a pomegranate, sliced it in half with his army knife and squeezed the red seeds directly into his mouth. The burst of sweetness overcame him with something he couldn't define. He squeezed his eyes closed and allowed them to fill with water. Upon opening them, he found himself looking at Boghos, who was studying him carefully.

"C'mon." He shrugged. The two walked the four kilometers back to Kessab, where they separated to cover ground, and began questioning every person they came upon. Finally, Asadour encountered an old woman from Kaladouran. He peered closely at the bent woman and saw that she was not really old. Her head was bare of any scarf, hair caked with dust; her toes poked through torn boots, the red yemeni leather of Kessab rubbed clean of color. But her wide brown eyes glistened from a face that was so haggard and lined, it had deceived Asadour—eyes that brightened at the sight of him!

"Asadour Karamardian! Praise God and blessings on you, young man. You are a sight for these eyes." Asadour bent to kiss her on each cheek and inhaling deeply, he gathered the courage to ask the inevitable question. He was spared the effort.

"I'm so sorry, dear boy, but your parents are gone. The children, too! May God rest their souls."

The ground below crumbled and no longer supported his weight. Dropping to his knees, Asadour felt the sharp stones pierce his skin and he relished the pain. Boghos appeared beside him, his face two shades lighter, having just taken in similar news. Sense of time suspended like a haze in which faces floated by on a current of foggy vapor. It was quite a while before the two cousins remembered that they were alive on a slab of solid earth with an old woman standing before them, studying their pale faces, and that she was of this life, in a world that still existed. Somehow, Asadour found words, but wasn't sure if he was speaking aloud or thinking them in his head.

"Have you seen anybody else? How have you managed?"

"I've walked from Amman. Yes, many of us in Amman have managed, thanks be to your cousin Shoushan, her talent for cooking, and the British army that took the camp early. On the way to Amman we stopped at camp in Homs. Asadour, I saw your Louisa there. In Homs!"

With the weightlessness of energy, the kind of energy that can renew life like a crack of thunder or flash of lightening,

Asadour was standing straight, kissing the woman named Ana, and bolting up the hill towards the road that led east. Boghos hurriedly trailed behind, calling out.

"Where are you headed, Asadour?"

Asadour did not look back but called over his shoulder, "To Homs! Of course!"

INTERLUDE

FACES OF 1911
Aurora, New York - 1991

AUTHOR

The moment he saw the photo, he burst into tears. It was August of 1991, and my cousin Ilene and family had arrived from Detroit to my parents' home on the lakeshore at Aurora, New York. This was some fifteen miles directly north of the old salt plant at Myers, and was where our family reunions had been convening every August since 1972. The last time the Detroit family contingency had come some years before, had been the only time I'd met 'little Alice.' The Karagozian-Hills were discussing their route through Canada as we all converged next to a mantelpiece in the dining room. Ilene whipped out the gift, the treasured photo she had discovered among Aunt Martha's things after she died, and propped it on the mantle so we could all look at once. As she presented it to my father, naming the people in it, George Peter found himself gazing at the face of his grandfather, Bedros (Peter), for the first time in his life. And naturally, my father, so connected to the ancestral soul and becoming more sentimental with every passing year, completely lost it.

Martha had evidently kept the photo hidden from anyone her entire life. It is unclear when she obtained it. Could she have brought it with her from Beirut in 1920? Ilene was Martha's only granddaughter. When she found it, she took the photo directly to Aunt Alice, still living in Detroit, to identify the faces. Alice knew these faces well.

Standing in back is Nishan and his wife, also an Injejikian by birth. I received conflicting versions of her name from the first generation witnesses. Uncle Leo called her Latiffe, which I instinctively want to reject; it is an Arab name, not Armenian. Perhaps it was used in the Arabic community of Latakia, who knows? Another called her Louise. I chose to compromise with a version of that, Lousine. But I cannot help but imagine that, if she lived, she may have become "Latiffe" in the Turkish household into which she was stolen.

The couple is flanked by Mary on the left, and Marta on the right, who appears approximately eleven-years-old. Seated before them on the left is someone holding a basket in front of their torso to shield them from view, a tradition to honor deceased members of a family—likely Tzaghir. Seated to the right is Bedros, the father. And on his lap, as well as on the hidden lap, are seated three children—two girls and a boy—who appear beautiful to me. According to Alice, the children (and their mother) were stolen by the Turks and, though carefully searched for, were never found.

With math and sleuthing, I calculate the photo to have been taken around 1911. All of the brothers except Nishan had, by then, left the country, if only barely. Mary, a teen, was undoubtedly running the household. Her stoic face strikes me as no-nonsense; the black and white photography does not do justice to the rumors of her beauty. Nor can it confirm the redness of her hair or that of her "red-haired" father, Bedros. Red hair was not unusual within the Armenian Kingdom of Cilicia. Kessab and Latakia hold special places in history among the era of Crusaders and their alliance with Christian Armenians. And many centuries earlier, some of Armenia's fiercest princes (Tiridates, Tigranes) were known to have thick or "wild" red hair, so the gene clearly predated European arrivals to Cilicia and the Levant. I find myself fantasizing about where the photo may have been taken. At the family home in Latakia? Or the summer ancestral home at Kaladouran? Kessab? Since I was a kid, Kessab is the name that represents anything that came *before*.

My introduction to Kessab had been, quite literally, a visual gateway. A hand-painted sign that spelled 'Kessab Acres' arched over the gated entrance to Uncle Mitch's horse farm in Groton, New York. It looked just like ranch signs in black and white western films of the era, and promised the thrill of horses and delirious excitement when we drove through it on any given Sunday. On one of those days, I expressed my curiosity.

"What does that word *Kessab* mean, Dad?"

"It is the name of Jido's hometown in the old country. Kessab, in Syria."

Only ten years old, and as yet unaware of the Armenian connection, the magic had, nonetheless, been planted—my quest for Camelot. When I was later made aware of Jido's ancestry, and read everything I could find about Kessab, I learned that the town and its surrounding villages had, for centuries, subsisted exclusively on agriculture—even with land unsuitable for farming. Silk, tobacco, and oil were taken by merchants to Aleppo, Adana, Beirut, Cyprus, and Egypt while smaller quantities of cereals, fruits, and livestock were grown for local consumption. Kessabtsis were also uniquely known for trades and crafts like coppersmithing, white embroidery from silk cocoons and, I would eventually learn, the Karamardian trade of shoemaking— specifically, red leather shoes called *yemeni*.

The Armenian villages along the Mediterranean coast of Cilicia were well established by the time the Crusaders arrived. Created as Cilician Armenia, and later abandoned, by the Byzantine Empire, these communities had been governed by their own princes and nobility until the Seljuk invasion of 1045. The region of Jabal Aqra, or Mount Cassius, was inhabited solely by Armenians and the principal village was Kessab (also spelled throughout history as Kasab, Casap, and Kesab). There are medieval ruins that indicate active monastic institutions, clearly a haven for the crusaders when they found refuge in the area, and accounts from crusaders such as King Boudoin II of Jerusalem and Count Pons of Tripoli who wrote that they found refuge among the Armenians of Kessab when attacked by Turkish bandits in 1119. A combination of research and calculated guess places the Karamardians in Kessab from at least around the 11th century, and originally from the Lake Van region of Anatolia.

As the 20th century took hold, unceasing events rocked the region. 1895 massacres against Armenians were repeated in 1909 and, by 1911, emigration of Armenian men to the

Americas (mostly South America, cousin Garbis tells me) was the norm. The year 1911 haunts me for more than one reason. Another photo, gifted to me before her death, by one of the California Karamardians, Aunt Mary of Tarzana, seems to mark the same year.

It is of five male students, taken either just before embarking for America, or for some celebration such as a wedding or graduation in the U.S. All five men wear a carnation in their lapel and fine leathered, two-toned shoes. The five boys from Kessab had sailed west to study in America, in Rochester, NY, it was said. Seated in the front row are two first cousins, Asadour Karamardian (right) and Boghos Boghossian (left) before they enlisted with the Legionnaires. Asadour had indeed come to study in America, and logic suggests that he remained longer than planned because war had broken out. (He also registered for the draft in Detroit in 1917.) I had learned how this "cousin" Asadour (Stepan's father) had been instrumental in my family's wellbeing. According to her daughter-in-law, Seta, Louisa had always said she and Asadour were engaged for seven years. Asadour, therefore, became engaged to Louisa in 1911.

That same year, I am told, Boghos had been offered the opportunity to study abroad by his father's employer and American sponsor. (Cousin Boghos, nicknamed 'Ingeles' for the remainder of his life, was Aunt Mary's father—that is Mary, wife of Aram and granddaughter of another Mary Karamardian). It was determined among the family, for some reason, that Asadour might accompany him and engage in studies as well, at Rochester, New York. They traveled with Josef Churukian and his brother (first name unknown, but possibly Vahan) and a boy named Boujikian, nicknamed Khasir because he was short. These are the three boys standing in the photo.

Before leaving, Asadour kissed his betrothed Louisa goodbye and the five Kessab boys departed Syria. It took no stretch of imagination to see that Leo (Manas), Jido's high strung brother, probably traveled with them. He arrived at Myers about the same time, in close proximity to Rochester, and by the same train network across central New York.

For me, 1911 is a year that haunts. It represents something in and for my family. Perhaps, it was the moment when the family was last intact and safe, when dreams were real and unencumbered, when so much innocence was yet to be lost. The photos from that year feel like a bookmark to the story of the Karamardian family in the old country (though clues continued to miraculously appear). My father's tears for the image of his grandfather, Bedros, whose name he wore as his surname (Peter), will never leave me.

Bedros Karamardian family circa 1911

Left to right in back: Mary Karamardian, Latife/Lucine (wife of Nishan) Injejikian Karamardian*, Nishan Karamardian, Bedros Karamardian, Marta (Martha) Karamardian

Front: children of Nishan Zaha, Mary, and son (name unknown)*

*Children and mother taken by Turkish gendarmes, forever lost

CHAPTER 9

SOLDIERS
Homs, Syria - 1918

LOUISA

In October, just as we had become accustomed to the settled dust that caked our faces and clothes—the color of our hair no longer identifiable—the dust rose up again, came alive, swirling into enormous cloud formations that rained fresh soot onto camp. It was accompanied with the thunder of marching boots that played a ragged beat buried in a consistent boom. The British appeared like the knights of the Crusades that I teach stories of to the older students. Columns of uniformed men in casual formation marched right into our midst so swiftly that all visibility was voided in minutes. Since we could see nothing for a time, the students and I just stood gaping until the battalion had worked its way through to the far end of camp and the soil particles began to fall back to earth, clearing the air for the scene to reopen. We could just barely see boots and backsides, and rifles angled from their shoulders. Although my heart instinctively lightened a bit, I was unsure what to do next.

It was determined that for most of us in camp, it was not yet safe to return home even if we could manage to do so. My duty was to my students, so I decided to take life one day, and one lesson, at a time. By luck or miracle or both, an answer—the next step—will present itself, I told myself. So with soldiers milling about the encampment and adding to the ruckus and noise and soot, I focused on maintaining some degree of normality for the children. I had been teaching history to the oldest students; now all my senses screamed that we were living it and I sought to portray this without frightening them. In spite of their excitement, most of them were too malnourished to engage in physical activities or distractions. Daily life for Mary, Garabet, and me continued a monotonous routine that was now, at least, fused with less fear, our only option to live each day within the realm of our current reality.

In December, it occurred to me that with increased provisions—thanks to the Brits—and improved health, the children might be up to preparing a holiday presentation to brighten the days of this cold, dark month. It would be presented on the New Year and again for the Christmas celebration on the 6th of January. I kept them an extra hour each class and taught them the only poems and songs I could recite from memory. I was told by a commander, who stopped by to observe our progress, that missionaries were again teaching in Beyruth and I fervently wished that we had them in our midst, along with primers and hymnals and chalk tablets. However, we would manage. Another young girl, herself from Homs, had finished the primary school and was able to assist me, taking the younger children for walks and drawing mathematical symbols in the dust. The plan helped my siblings and me stay focused in the day and not lose ourselves to thoughts and memories of our parents, or the growing realization that we had nowhere to return to.

During the third week of this new schedule, the children and I sang one of the songs together and it seemed to be taking shape. I was rather pleased and decided to dismiss the group a few minutes early. Mary helped me to gather the British-issued blankets some children had left behind, attempt to fold the rough, brown sheets of fabric, and find a place for their safekeeping. I glanced up at the backs of the retreating children as they worked their way through camp in search of what few family had survived to care for them.

As I was about to turn back to my task, I noticed a soldier standing alone at the edge of our area, looking about. He stood out because his uniform was a slightly different color beneath its coat of dust from the British ones I had become accustomed to, and also rather ragged and torn, as if the man had not been issued a replacement after major battle. While I pondered the observation, it occurred to me that the soldier had ceased to look about the camp and was staring directly at me.

I should have been uneasy, embarrassed, or at least appropriately demure; at the very least I should have turned away my eyes, but something held me in place. I froze and remained so, even as he began walking slowly toward me. Very slowly, as if in slow motion. His walk seemed familiar; is he a relative? Still too far away to make out his face, I was now mesmerized, even allowing myself to fantasize that something special, an angel perhaps, was advancing to bestow on me news of a loved one. I remained rooted in place and allowed the seconds to tick by as he came closer, and closer, dust swirling about him and suddenly I could see his face. It couldn't be! My beloved was across the big ocean on another continent and the man walking towards me was a soldier of, of what I did not know. When he spoke, I knew.

"Louisa…" It was his voice; even choked, there was no doubt. It was his face, though different, aged. It had been more than seven years. He was running now. I somehow found my feet, too, as I vaguely heard Mary from behind me call out, the tremor in her voice betrayed an absence of recognition, or understanding.

"Louisa?!"

I gave no thought to my behavior, not as a teacher, as a woman, as an unmarried Armenian. I flew into Asadour's arms, both of us crying, clinging to one another. Mary and Garabet approached timidly, and Asadour knelt before them in the dirt.

"Why, Mary! You're no longer a girl!" He was looking up at my teenaged sister whose face I'd never before seen blush so deeply as it now did. He then turned in wonderment to Garabet; my mother had only just given birth to my brother when Asadour departed Syria.

"Well, young man, I am so happy to finally meet you. I thank you for taking good care of my fiancé, your sister." I was taken aback when Garabet immediately threw his arms about Asadour's neck, something I'd never seen him do except with my mother or me.

It amazes me that after years of self-reliance—of discovering that I am able to keep myself and my siblings alive with sheer determination—I could so easily slip into the emotional and physical relief found within the protection and care of my future husband. All four of us exhaled; we smiled for days to come. Not only did the family unit now include Asadour, but we gratefully deferred to his natural guidance and leadership of it. As a family, we decided to stay through Christmas and then begin the walk back to Kaladouran and Kessab. As a family, we cried for our parents and his, Asadour's siblings, and all of the villagers who had left Kaladouran with us but not survived the ordeal. Asadour confessed to me that he and his cousin had abandoned the Gamavor unit when they witnessed betrayal in Cilicia. It amazed me that he decided to approach the commander at the camp and discuss what he had done, risking punitive action and the possibility of being turned over to the French.

Instead of punishment, the commander praised his efforts for the battle he and his compatriots had fought at Arara, telling him, "The bravery of you Armenian lads allowed the whole regiment to pivot and chase the Ottomans all the way to Aleppo and beyond! It was the cover you provided that turned around the campaign and allowed the win." Furthermore, the Brit said, the French had dissolved La Legion Armenienne in Cilicia, rendering the four battalions no longer useful. So he had not abandoned what didn't exist.

The small battalion of troops that remain in Homs joined us for the Christmas celebration on January 6th, offering their own voices to the Protestant hymns I had learned from the missionaries at Kessab and taught the children at Homs. It was a joyous day indeed. But not the most joyous. The best day had already occurred (on the last day of the year) when the commander officiated a wedding ceremony for Asadour and me. So we returned to Kessab as husband and wife, as well as guardians of my sister and brother.

CHAPTER 10

HOME

Kessab, Syria - 1918

LOUISA

On the slow, long walk home we passed by what I guessed to be the spot where my father had fallen in death. There were bones still strewn everywhere on the ridge and paths, some gnawed clean by animals, some partially buried in frantic attempts during the march. I also saw a marker under a mulberry tree and wondered aloud about Shoushan's baby. In Hama and several other towns, we saw ruins of monasteries and castles from the time of the Crusades, not unlike our own ruins on Mount Aqra. Once we had passed the cut-off road to Ladehkiya, we even met some Kessabtsis and other Armenians headed north to Cilicia. All were coming from the south. Few came from the east and we eventually learned why: it was the road from Deir al Zor, the desert from where almost any Armenian who had been taken, was not fated to return.

Finally, we quite literally stumbled into Kessab; we were tired, hungry, but happy and determined to rebuild our lives. But even as more people of Kessab straggled back to town, many were repeatedly attacked by bands of Turks from over the mountain and from the east. So forty men who had returned from serving in La Legion Armenienne met together and distributed what weapons they had brought home from the war. They set up patrols and called themselves Gamavor, in honor of their bravery as war volunteers. The group included cousin Boghos, who everyone now called either Ingeles or Paul and also, one of four Karamardian cousins named Khatchig who returned from Egypt. He'd been in the camp at Port Said when Asadour was there, though the two did not see one another. He, too, was determined to join the Gamavor. The Gamavors managed to repel constant attacks from outlying areas on Kessab and the villages, remaining vigilant for more than five years. It was only for the efforts of these menfolk that life was able to resume. Asadour's plan was to take us back to Amirka once things were settled here.

Meanwhile, we returned to Giragos and Kitcha's home in Kaladouran where Asadour whipped the garden into shape. We made a little shrine for his family under the grapevine trellis where I found myself having conversations with my friend and late sister-in-law, Louise. Asadour wanted to wire his cousin Hovsep in Michigan to inform him what he had learned of the family but, as yet, there was no wiring service in place. New things came to light daily as people drifted back into town. It became apparent that only about a third of Kessab residents survived to return. The people of Kaladouran fared slightly better; forty percent survived. Most of these returned from Amman.

Joy of joys, cousin Shoushan, with her husband Shamo Titizian, were already next door to us in the village. Most of her family had managed to stay alive in the camp at Amman where they had been moved after our meeting in Homs. The British had taken Jordan early on so they had suffered under German control for only one year. Shoushan cooked for the camp and made certain her family was sufficiently fed throughout the three years. But her eldest daughter, Frieda, had succumbed to a fever illness, and her infant… well, we had seen the mulberry tree on the trek from Homs.

We received a letter from Asadour's cousin, Elisa, from an orphanage in Constantinople; thanks be to God for her survival. She addressed her letter to Asadour Karamardian, her own father; she may have been in that hopeful state of prayer, having no definite knowledge of the fate of her parents. Thankfully, the letter was brought to my husband of the same name. Elisa wrote that when Armenian priests came to free her and some other girls, she discovered her brother, Vahan, to be in another orphanage, where he was to remain. Asadour consulted with his cousin Khatchig and sent word to her that Khatchig would send her the fare. But she wrote again, and graciously explained that she decided, for now, to remain and continue her studies. She said she would return to Kessab after acquiring a degree. What a brave young woman, I thought. She had no family left to return to, poor girl, so I supposed it was a wise decision for her future. My sweet, favorite pupil deserved her education!

The only other Karamardian who returned to town shook us to the core from his appearance and trauma. That is how we learned about Deir al Zor and that most of the people from

Kessab proper were marched to its desert, and what everyone now calls the death camp. Few even made it as far as the desert camp, including Serop. Now a young man, he walked into Kessab like a ghost. He had been on the march when the Turkish guards who were supposed to protect them from Kurdish bandits, instead invited a group of Kurdish horse riders to attack the whole clump of the Armenians trudging along on the path. The group were stabbed and bludgeoned. His mother, father, and brother Stepan had fallen from their wounds and actually fell on top of him! Serop could barely breathe from the weight and, for hours, was much too frightened to move. He lay on the ground beneath the corpses of his beloved family for close to a day before he attempted to push them off from his body. Just as he was emerging, a family of Kurds came along to rob the bodies of the many corpses strewn along the road. When they encountered Serop among the dead they took pity on him and fed him. The family cared for him for two weeks. When they felt him strong enough, they pointed him south towards Lebanon, to where they believed he might run into British troops. With the bit of nourishment the Kurds had provided, he managed the walk, over days, to the vicinity of British troops and found protection.

Gradually, bits of normal life were strung together, although we saw little of Asadour when he patrolled the mountain. I found rice and lentils stored in Kitcha's underground pantry and Shoushan lent me some cracked wheat. Meals became a delight. Soon we would rebuild and open the schools, now closed. But on a Sunday, as I scraped grains of pilaf from the pot and put it to soak, voices outside called to Asadour and I raced to the door. There stood an elderly man; indeed, I could not understand how it was that he walked on his feet, and he was holding the arm of a young girl, perhaps a teen, it was hard to tell. As I peered more closely at his face, I could see that I had known him years before, from this very village. It seemed he was old then, but now…

"Why, Hagop Aslanian! I have not seen you in some years. Welcome."

I motioned them into the house. Someone had raced to Kessab looking for Asadour, and now he came running, which surprised me. He burst into the house, his face alive.

"Marta! Marta-jan!" He was embracing the girl instantly, though I noticed her wince at his touch. Could it be? I had not recognized her at first glance because I was focused on Hagop. But now I studied the face of the young girl I recalled and could see it truly was Marta. And it was now clear that it was she who could barely stand and whose face was paler than a white dove. When she slipped into the closest chair, we did not see at first that she had fainted.

Marta was so ill that it took many days to extract any detail at all. Hagop gave us some clues. He had been living in a village near Iskenderun and managed to evade the deportations. Due to his age and his living alone, the Turks had simply overlooked him in the mostly Muslim village. The only Armenians around were either slaves or old like him. When he saw Marta at the well one day, he recognized her from Kaladouran, from the summers of her childhood. He continued to look for her and to try to talk to her, though she was frightened of him—of anything and everyone, it seemed to him—and did not speak back to him whenever he tried to approach her at the well. He thought she looked so forlorn that she must have been stolen. When the war ended, he looked for her in earnest after he saw people from the Red Cross go to Turkish homes looking for Armenian children that had been taken. The doctor's home where she lived—she said she worked for him—was modest and he watched to see if she would emerge. She did come to the well one day, carrying a small bag. She walked straight to Hagop and, in Turkish, asked if her could help her. She said the doctor told her she could go, and where to look for Armenians in the city. But she dared not. Such a frightened girl she was, showing no joy in her release or any knowledge of the world around her or the war that had been raging. Hagop told her he would take her to Kessab, a trek that neither of them were in condition to undertake. Yet here they were!

We took them both in, of course. Marta was too ill to swallow more than broth for many days. It was weeks until she could eat some pilaf and a bit of lamb. Her weakness alarmed me. But more alarming was her silence. Marta had not yet spoken a word and I began to wonder if she had forgotten our language. At first, it seemed she did not understand what was said to her. Eventually, I saw her eyes flicker at the words when I made a point to clarify the names of dishes I put in front of her. She was recognizing food names first, then our names. With time and strength, came the tears.

She cried and cried at times, as if only now expelling her experience of the past four years. And with her tears, slowly came her words. As if the crying returned her native Kessabtsi, Marta began to talk, just a little and with limited vocabulary.

She managed to tell us of seeing Nishan shot in front of her. When we asked about the rest of the family, she burst into sobs and stammered, "Th-they are Turks now!"

I tried to gently prod more information from her over time. When I first asked her how she came to be living with the Turkish doctor, she shut down, sobbing but otherwise mute. She seemed unable, perhaps unwilling, to provide information. Mostly I let her be. When I pressed her she seemed at a loss for the words. Perhaps, she could not remember enough Armenian yet. But one time, when I asked about Lousine and the children, she whispered, "They went in the cart. I went in the wrong one." And cried again, softly.

The fourth time we spoke of it, I asked, "Marta-jan, where did the cart take you?" She was silent for an interminable time and I decided to drop the subject. But then I heard her small voice say, "Slave camp…" and that was the end of it.

The poor darling. On the march I had heard the screams in the night of young girls dragged away from their families. I had seen mothers draw dirt lines all over the faces of their pretty daughters to make them ugly. I was the luckiest one. At least, of the survivors.

Asadour wrote to Hovsep, of course. The wire service in Ladehkiya had finally opened. Hovsep would reach Mary and her brothers. My heart broke for my husband, for his responsibility to his family, when he gently tried to persuade Marta.

"Come Marta-jan, you must get well. Your sister and brothers are alive. If you wish to see them again, you must get well." Her face did light up a little when her sister, Mary, was mentioned, but generally she was unresponsive. It seemed most logical to send her to Amirka, to rejoin her family, but she was in no shape to travel. And it could take a long time to get the papers and the passage from her brothers, yet Marta surprised us both by saying, "I want to go to school." So Asadour walked to Ladehkiya to find the Red Cross, and also to see about schooling, since the schools in Kessab had not yet opened. "My old school," she had added, which we assumed was in Ladehkiya, where she last lived.

The mission school in Ladehkiya was still closed and would reopen in a year or so. There was no other option for now, except to send her to the missionaries who had remained in Beyruth. And so, Asadour saved up for two train fares from Ladehkiya and, when she recovered, delivered Marta to the Beyruth Mission School. He was taken by complete surprise when she raced inside the building, smiling for the very first time since her return from Turkey. He soon learned that it had been here that she went to study after Mary's abduction. She had taken the train each week for a year to the Beyruth Mission School and returned to Nishan's home on the weekends.

Meanwhile, the Red Cross began communicating with her brothers in Michigan, U.S., to apply for papers for her, a process that took two years. Finally, passage was secured from Beyruth to Le Havre, France and New York. I studied the route and plan with an ulterior motive; we hoped to follow that path in a few years. But before her departure to France, Asadour received another wire from the Red Cross in Beyruth. This time the news was alarming. Marta was gone! She had disappeared two weeks before. The staff suspected she might have headed home to Kessab and hoped we could verify this.

Fortunately, praise be to God, they located her within hours of sailing, in just enough time to board the freighter. Astonishingly, Marta and another girl, who bore tattoos on her arm, had hidden themselves in a cemetery near the docks for the whole two weeks. It was determined they were so frightened of being stolen again before the ship sailed, and desperate to get on that freighter unmolested, that they had bonded in hiding. The intensity of such fear left me humbled and speechless.

For myself, I looked forward to our own travels to Amirka, where Asadour said we all would flourish, not just to witness Marta's recovery after reuniting with her siblings, but for the sake of my own siblings and future children. There was little hope here and still no peace to count on. Our parents would surely approve, under the circumstances, were they alive to render an opinion.

CHAPTER 11

EDUCATION

Constantinople, Turkey - 1918

ALICE

My far-off dream, the one I kept tucked deep in my sleep, has come true. Some Armenian priests came and called all the Armenians to the big room. They wrote our names down. Our real names! I said mine in Armenian: "Elisa Karamardian." Just like I memorized and remembered. The name, too, emerged from deep in my dreams. I don't know for how long I had not uttered the language of home.

The priests were very serious, and I did not know what they planned. Now almost fourteen, I attempted to ask the question, but the priest I addressed did not respond. I waited. There was nothing more to do in this place. Some of the girls were Armenian like me. But most were not and I did not trust myself to know any of them intimately, even when I had learned Turkish well. But after two weeks, the priests came back; they stood in the hall again and called our names in Armenian. I stepped forward when my name was called.

The priest said, "Go and get your things. Everything. Then return here at once."

They took me and ten other girls to another orphanage in the city, this one for Armenians. Once again, we lined up in a large hall. First the priests blessed and anointed us. There were many more children there and after the blessing, all the children of this place joined in the big room. I don't know how but suddenly, a woman from my old neighborhood appeared in that room. She said she was an aunt. I knew her face but couldn't recall her name.

She looked right at me and she called out, "Elisa! Your brother is here!" Imagine the joy that spread through my whole body after my mind caught up with the shock.

Poor Vahan did not much remember me. He was not yet in kindergarten when we were taken. But I held him like he was my own baby, and he knew my name and said it over and over. And then, maybe from all my happiness, I came alive with memories, and I asked him, "Is Vartouhi here?" but he only looked at me, puzzled, as if he couldn't remember.

Then they took him away. They took him to another orphanage that they called 'Black Eyes' and I stayed in this new one. Missionaries came and questioned everyone. They told us the war was over, that we could try to find our families. But there was nobody looking for me.

The classes now were strong, and I began to learn classics, even Greek. That year I finished my regular schooling, but I really wanted to study more, and deeper. I thought about Kessab and Ladehkiya. I remembered my family and mentally went through all the names I could think of: my father and many more Asadours (three—no, four cousins named Asadour Karamardian); there was grandfather Khatchig, and, let's see, four cousins named Khatchig. Marta, where could she be? I remembered Mary was taken by Turks. Cousin Serop, who was my age, and his older brother Stepan. My two Frieda cousins. Ossanan, Rachel. Uncles Giragos, Marderos, Shamo, oh, and Shoushan and her Marian. Gulenia, Manas… I was remembering!

A teacher helped me. I addressed my letter to 'Asadour Karamardian' at Kessab. Anyone might receive it, anyone who was there. I wrote my name, where I was, and asked about my parents and Vartouhi. There was nothing more to say, really. And nothing to do but wait.

A letter came back from Asadour, my cousin in Kaladouran village. He wrote only of who had returned. It was a very short list: Shoushan and all her children except for Frieda, Serop, and Khatchig the eldest cousin. There were no more. No word of Mayrig, Vartouhi, or Marta. He told me that I could come home to Kessab. That Khatchig will send the passage for the train. I lay in my bed the night I received the letter and I tried so hard to think. I pictured coming home to Kessab with no Mayrig, no Hayrig. No Vartouhi or Vahan there. No mother, father, sister, or brother. I thought about school. And how little Kessab was. I wanted only to study. What else was there for me?

The next day I asked the teacher I like best for a meeting. I asked her what studies I might be able to do to learn further than the basics I had completed. She told me I could study for a degree, to teach, and that I could stay there at the orphanage to complete my studies. I decided it was the best option for me, now. Besides, I could wait for Vahan to graduate and perhaps take him home with me. So I wrote to Asadour. I thanked him so much for the letter. I told him I will remain in Constantinople and study, finish my degree; after, I will come to Kessab and be a teacher there.

CHAPTER 12

SISTER

Port Huron, MI - June 1918

HENNA (JOHN)

Once we were headed up the hill from Port Hune, I caught my breath at the first sight of the lake. At a certain spot it was visible below, glittering under the sun. Sometimes it seemed to be grumpy, like a mad person, when clouds would cover it with dark shadows. But today it shone and shimmered with little sparkles floating on the top. Pa told me it is miles away, but from way up here, I imagine I can reach out and touch it, or maybe sail out into the sky with the hawks and slowly float down into that magical pool. Pa also said that on the other side of the lake is a whole other country, *Kanadah*. Ma said she feels like she lives inside a miracle when she rocks on the porch and looks out at big Lake Hune in the distance, just like back at Tubbha, where I was born. There, she said, you could walk to the water's edge at the bottom of the hill, to work in the plant or play in the park. This was confusing, but I asked no questions.

We came back to the farm today. The drive up the hill to the house was overgrown with bushes hanging over the edge and grasses popping up through grey stones that click under the horse's feet. When we pulled up to the small barn I leaped down, excited to say hello to the cow and maybe even circle round the house, but Ma yelled right away.

"Henna, don't you dare run off! Come right here and take your sister's hand and this basket! And watch Jake, for God's sake, before he runs to the field!"

I carefully took Zaha's hand, looked around for Jake but saw he was already darting up the porch steps to the house, so I gripped Ma's food basket with my other fingers. Zaha squeezed my hand and smiled up at me, melting my heart not for the first time that day. I wished she would stop doing that, it is very distracting sometimes. I looked over at Ma, dangling baby Susie on her hip while she reached back into the wagon to gather up shawls and the things left on the bench. When she straightened up and gazed at the horizon just above the lake, I could tell she was just as happy as me and Pa to be back home in Port Hune. So was Jake, who was racing round and round on the wraparound porch. I wished I could be the first inside, but he would surely beat me to it.

Pa sure has us moving around a lot, I thought. I remembered this place the most, but we went to Highland Park twice, and also to Flint for a while. Pa says it's because a small farm doesn't feed a whole family and he has to have other work, too. I guess he changes jobs a lot. It was fun to be in Highland Park because my cousin Albert was there to play with Jake and Aunt Mary and Uncle Leo came to our house a lot. Pa speaks with them in a language that's different than ours. Even Ma can't understand them. But we have more cousins in Port Hune because Uncle Moses lives here and he's got four boys—Mose, John, George, and Frank—and, when we play together, we get into a lot of trouble. Ma always yells, "Too many boys! It's not natural!" And Pa always laughs.

Pa worked for Ford in Highland Park. But he quit and that's why he said I have to go to school now. I really didn't understand.

That night we had our first meal back in the kitchen Ma loves. She was always looking out the window. She called it a luxury she didn't want to live without, that window and its view from on top of the world. The smell of fried lamb and onion gripped my stomach, and I strained for the food Ma was dishing out. She slapped my hand. Then Pa spoke to me.

"You will go tomorrow with Flora to the school in town," he said. Flora was the big girl next door; I wasn't scared of her, but I was scared of whatever this "school" was.

"You have to learn to read."

"Why? Do you read?" As soon as it slipped out of my mouth, I thought I might be in trouble. But I didn't mean to sass; I was curious. Pa was quiet for a good while. Ma and he looked at each other.

Then he looked straight at me. "You know how I was working at the Ford auto plant?" I nodded back, waiting.

"When I got the steel sliver in my toe, they put me to work in the mail room." I stared at him blankly. "Everything was fine for three months. Then they found out I couldn't read!"

"Oh." Now, I thought I understood. "So they made you leave the job!"

"No! They told me they would send me to school!" Yippee, I thought! Pa is going to go to school with me. I clapped my hands, but Pa looked at me sharply.

"'Never mind, I quit!' I said 'I don't have time for school!'"

My shoulders slumped to the table, my short-lived excitement squeezed out. Pa was gentle now.

"You see, Henna, I don't have time for school now because I have to work for you and your brother and sisters and your mother. But I went to school when I was a boy like you. I can write in my language and some others too, just not in Amirkan. You must learn to write in Een-glish, like all boys and girls in Amirka." Then he looked for a moment like he was thinking real hard and said, "If I could read Eenglish, I would have known that my ship sank."

Ma and I both looked at him; we had no idea what he was talking about. So he said, "I heard it in town today. Happened last summer. The *S.S. Carolina*, torpedoed by the Germans. Right off the shore of Noo Jursee, right here in Amirka. My ship from the islands."

The next morning Ma packed me some bread and leftovers in a pail and Flora came to the door to collect me. But I tell you, when I walked into the room filled with other kids where she left me, I couldn't understand anything that was happening. A teacher came toward me, and her lips were moving but the sounds she made were nothing I had heard before. She pulled me to a seat but the other children were also making strange sounds, so I sat there all morning afraid to speak or move.

When Flora took me home and was too far away to hear, I bawled. Ma shook her head and scolded me like she was mad. But I told her that the people were making funny noises and I couldn't understand a single word. Ma's face turned all funny and that night I heard her tell Pa, "It wasn't fair to him. He'll have to learn some words first."

And I didn't have to go back to that school! Not then. My birthday was coming in May and I would be six! Pa worked real early, baking bread at the salt plant, and when he came home in the afternoons, I helped him plant the gardens. On Sundays, I watched Jake and Zaha for Ma when she was cooking or feeding Susie. Zaha liked to help too. She was only two years old, but she would pull the little stool to the sink and stand on it and help Ma wash the dishes. It made Ma laugh so hard. Ma made a smeed (farina) cake for my birthday and when the priest and the Syrians came for mass on Sunday, they all sang to me. I was happy as could be. I let Zaha and Jake blow out the candles with me. It was some sort of other holiday, too, so Pa set up planks on sawhorses for tables and the Syrians brought platters and had a big feast in our yard to the side of the barn where the view of the lake is best.

After that Zaha got sick. A doctor came to the house once. He called her little Lo-ra. I asked Ma why and she said that "Loh-rah" is Zaha's Amirkan name. I asked her if I have an Amirkan name and she looked down at me surprised.

"Of course! It's Jaahn." Then she sniffed and looked real worried.

There was a black spot on Zaha's face and it did not go away. Ma and Pa spoke in whispers, and Zaha stayed in the bed a lot of time. Our room was big and Zaha and Jake and I all had one bed. Susie, the baby, sometimes slept in the crib where little Jirgis used to sleep. Sometimes she cried too much and Ma took her to her own bed. But after a month, Ma set up a little bed in her room for Zaha, separate from us. Susie came back to the crib in our room, like a swapping of sisters. I missed the sound of Zaha's sweet breathing in the bed between me and Jake. But I didn't miss her talking. All the time. Zaha talked more than even Jake and me. Ma said she talked like an eight-year-old, which is way more old than me!

It was June. I know because the planting was finished. But it must have been Sunday because Pa was already up and out, in the barn, I guess. I heard Zaha call and I heard Ma go to the bedroom so I got up and walked in my bare feet to the bedroom doorway looking for them. I stopped still and quiet when I saw Ma tenderly bent over my sister, who was speaking, real sweetly.

"Get Pa. It's time for me to go," I heard her say the words before Ma started to scream.

"I'll get the doctor!" But Zaha looked intently at Ma's face like she was waiting for her to get quiet again.

"He'll never make it." Then, clear as anything, she said, "Don't be sad, Mother. I'm going to the most beautiful place you ever saw!" and I flew out the door to find Pa, fast as I could. I didn't know what else to do. But Zaha died in Ma's arms before I got to him.

Our house on the hill was plenty sad for a long time. I heard Ma cry in her room every night and every morning that she wasn't busy with something in particular. We buried Zaha in a place under a tree where you could see the lake good and clear with no trees blocking the sparkles on the water. Ma said she deserved the most beautiful spot in her new world. Her third birthday came on August 21st and even Pa cried that day.

When we sat at dinner that night, I saw Pa pat Ma's hand before he said, "Helen, you'll make more!" She smiled that night but the next day the postman knocked on the door.

When Ma went to open it, I heard him say, "Oh, Mrs. Peter, I'm so sorry to hear of your daughter passing. I hope it wasn't the pretty one…" and Ma wailed all over again.

Ma's belly grew really big again that summer. But when the baby came out, it was dead too. Ma sighed and said, "God meant for him to keep Zaha company. In heaven."

One thing changed that made me happy. The harvest started coming in, and Pa spent lots of nights before supper selling vegetables from the back of the cart. I already helped by milking our cow every morning, and Pa took the milk to sell to a grocer on his way to work at the salt plant. On Saturdays, he hitched the horse and drove the cart into the hills to a neighborhood of people that really like him and this year he decided to take me along. Ma complained that she needed my help, but Pa said, "Helen, let the boy have some minutes!" And that was that. Funny, though, he spoke a whole other language with the people on the hill; not Syrian, like us, and not the language he spoke with his brothers. These people called him José. I asked him if it was Amirkan. He said, "No, it is Spanish." I guess he is the smartest Pa in the world.

A letter came in June. It came from the old country, from Uncle Asadour; that's Pa's cousin who stayed with us when I was younger than Jake is now. I remember him, when I was four. He liked to touch my head and scramble my hair. Now there was so much excitement, Pa whooped it up. The letter made him happy again. Then Pa took the train to Highland Park to see his brothers and Aunty Mary. Ma said the letter was about his sister in the old country. Another sister.

"She's alive! She's coming!"

CHAPTER 13

SHOE SHOP
Port Huron, MI - 1920

JOHN (HENNA)

It seemed like a whole long time that we waited for my aunt to come from the old country. Ma said it was a whole year. When I asked her questions, she began to answer them, like she really wanted to talk about things with someone and I was glad to be the one. Ma went on telling me more and more stories about the old country. First, she told me that Pa's family was mostly dead. By the blood-soaked hands of dirty Turks. And that they stole his sisters. But my Aunt Mary was rescued and is now blessed with my cousins Albert and the littler ones, and now God has produced another miracle. Marta is also saved and papers are being made and she would be coming to Port Hune to live with us. Under her breath, Ma also said that she hoped that Marta could talk more than her sister. I don't know what that meant but before I could ask, she shushed me out the door, stories done for now.

On the day of the firelights, we had a big party for all the Syrians. I helped Pa set up planks on the sawhorses to make long tables in the field next to the house. All the ladies came with platters and the feast began before the sun went away. It was July 4th and we got to see the fire show burst open over the lake right from home! I saw firelights when we lived in Highland Park, from a big park by the lake there, too. Pa says it's the same lake as this, that's how big it is, more like a sea than a lake. That time we were up close to the edge of the lake with so many people I was afraid to wander away and get lost, which, of course, Jake did more than once so that Pa gave us both such a spanking! It was impossible to hold Jake back or give him orders. He could forget in a minute and disappear, and cause so much trouble I could shake him. But this time the sparkles were different; even though they were far away, they were more magical, with designs unfolding in the blackness. I didn't have to crane my neck to see them above my head; I could just sit back and enjoy the colors burst apart in the sky while all the grown-ups aahed.

When the winds got really cold and snow came, Ma said Marta would be coming soon. But first she made another brother for us. Nishan was born the 13th of November. Ma said we were naming him for Pa's brother who the Turks killed. Other people called our new baby Mitch, his Amirkan name, I guess. I thought about how lucky we all are to have two names. Except Susie. She is just "Susie" and she turned two in the summer. She runs everywhere, and I have to chase after her now that Ma has another baby keeping her busy. Then Pa said he should go to New York to bring Marta to Port Hune, and Ma got so mad she stamped her foot.

"You can't leave me here to fend alone now with ta kids, ta baby, cooking, and keep ta firewood in, too! What are you thinking, Yussef? And it's Christmastime!"

"I just don't know if I should trust Manas. Khatchig is leaving for California at the goddam wrong time, to the wrong direction." Pa's brothers sometimes seemed complicated to me, based on things I heard Pa grumble about. But Ma got the last word about Uncle Leo.

"It's time for that brother to step up. You're gonna have to tell Leo to bring her." And it was settled. Pa took the train to Detroit to work it out with Uncle Leo.

She came to us on the Amirkan Christmas day. Pa had taken Ma and us to church and told us we would have a present. Then Pa dragged in a spruce tree and set it up right inside the house! The next morning we got up and waited. Ma cooked all day, all the things she always cooked plus some other things she learned from Aunty Mary that she said Aunty Marta would like. "Her own kind of shah-di-yeh," she mumbled. The house smelled wonderful. Pa even baked bread for us; I loved watching him throw the dough into the air and catch it all flattened out. I helped stack some wood and after that Pa paced around, looking for things to do. He seemed nervous. Finally, he hitched the wagon and went to the train. When he came back, he had our new aunt and Uncle Leo with him, and the house filled up with that other language that only Pa and my uncles speak.

It filled up even more on the last day of the year because Aunty Mary and Uncle Ameen came with my boy cousins.

Holy Moly, this was the best holiday ever, especially when Aunty Mary and Aunty Marta hugged each other all day and all night. When I puffed up my courage and asked them why they hug all the time, they looked at each other and giggled. Then at the very same time, they said, "Because we're alive!" That was the only time I ever heard them laugh until I was old.

Well, we had the best foods and time for a whole week. Pa brought up his homemade whiskey from the basement where he kept his copper whiskey making thing that we kids were forbidden to go near. On the morning of Christmas, January 6th, there was a present for me under the pretty spruce tree that my aunts had decorated with tiny things they made from scraps and pinecones. There was a present for each of my cousins and for Jake and Susie, too: a little wooden cart and a doll. My present was wrapped in brown paper and when I opened it the whole room erupted with grown-ups talking at once. It was a car. A tiny toy car that looked oh, so fancy!

"It's the new model T, isn't it?" said Uncle Leo.

"That's exactly what it is!" said Uncle Ameen proudly. He was a machinist at Ford Motor Company and knew everything there is to know about "au-to-mo-beels," a word he sounded out real slow. Everybody oohed and aahed.

Uncle Leo poured a swig of Pa's brown whiskey into his glass and bellowed, "Well, you're already seven years old. You can't be without an au-to-mo-beel!" He said the word just like Uncle Ameen and everyone laughed. I couldn't imagine why the car magically came to be mine, but I ran off to play with it on the porch, snow and all. I was so glad that Jake and Susie had their own toys to play with and, just this once, left me alone.

Uncle Moses and Aunty Mary came that day, too, with my cousins Mussa, John, George, and the baby called Frank. Everybody talked a lot about cars and autos and then they got to talking about boats—ships.

Uncle Leo asked Aunty Marta, "What was your crossing like, Marta?

"The *S.S. Niagara*," she said like she was proud. "And I had a friend for the trip; I met Zarouhi at the Beyruth Red Cross. She is only seventeen and," for some reason Aunty Marta stopped talking normal and whispered the next thing, "she has tattoos on her arms." Nobody knew what to say about this. Uncle Moses asked what I was thinking but was too afraid to say.

"What were they from?" he asked.

"Turks," Aunty Marta said simply. And the room was silent for a minute. Then Pa told the aunties and uncles something he had told us before.

"Do you know the Germans torpedoed ships right off the coast of Noo Jursee in '18? The first one they hit was my ship!" He waited, and I could tell he wanted for everybody to ask what he meant. But they were quiet so he gave up and said, "The *S.S. Carolina*! I sailed it from Porto Rico when I came here. That was…"and he counted on his fingers, "twelve years ago."

At supper, Pa started telling a story about something that happened the week before, when he went to Highland Park to send Uncle Leo to New York and bring back Aunty Marta.

"We met him in the shoe shop. He's a nice fella. Also a survivor. From Yasgurt, Turkey. Went riding and when he came home, found his whole family dead. Got back on the horse and rode all the way to Greece." The uncles laughed at that, but not the aunties.

Someone snorted, "There must have been a boat somewhere in between," which made the uncles howl more.

"Khatchig was with us, too, before he caught his train west," Uncle Leo jumped in. I remembered then that Uncle Archie had moved very far away, to a place called Kalifornia. Pa said the doctor told him to go so his TB wouldn't come back. I don't know what that is, only that he caught it in the war and got sent home.

Pa and Uncle Leo were jumping all over each other to speak now, but Leo was first. "So all three of us got to approve."

"We told him our sister is coming next week. From the old country. Meet us here on the tenth and we'll bring her," said Pa. "Gazar… it's a good name, don't you think?"

"You can always count on meeting the best Armenians in a shoe shop," Uncle Leo added, like it was an important fact. Then he snickered, so maybe it was a joke. I'm not sure.

Aunty Marta didn't say anything, but she had a funny look on her face. I looked over at Aunty Mary and saw her nod like she approved of something. Then the aunties passed strange looks at each other. Pa seemed worried and got real soft and tender with Aunty Marta.

"Trust me, Marta-jan. You'd be safe and happy with this man. Just see if you like him. Just meet him. Give it a chance."

Aunty Marta said no more for a while. But suddenly she looked up and asked a question I couldn't understand, and Pa and my uncles just shook their heads. It was Uncle Leo who answered her, in Syrian, so we could all hear.

"Nobody has heard from Asadour since the letter we got before I sailed, Marta!" And they all got quiet, which made me scared. I was afraid to speak at the table of grownups, but couldn't help it.

I heard myself ask, "D-d-did Uncle Asadour die in the war?" I thought I might cry. I liked Uncle Asadour. There was a confused look that passed among everybody, but then Aunty Marta brightened her face and finally smiled. She bent down to me and spoke in perfect Syrian.

"Oh, no Henna-jan! You are thinking of our cousin Asadour, who you have met. He is safe in Kessab. He fought bravely in the war. He helped me come to you!"

"We have a brother, too, named Asadour," Pa was explaining, directly to me like I was as important as a grown-up, even though I was only seven. "He came to new country with me. But he went to Sowt Amirka, maybe Brasil. We don't know where he is." That night I dreamt of a lost Uncle named Asadour. He lived in a faraway place called Brasil. His eyes were lighter than Pa's or Ma's. I didn't know why.

When everyone packed up for the train back to Highland Park, Pa and Aunty Marta went with them for a few days. When they came back, Ma set up beds for Jake and me in the living room. Little Susie got to sleep in our bedroom with Aunty Marta. Aunty was different than Aunty Mary, not as pretty, but she was real kind and gentle. I got used to having her there, even though sometimes she started to cry, right out of nowhere. Ma didn't seem to mind at all, which really surprised me. She did not approve when we cried. Aunty Marta speaks our Syrian language real good. One day they were in the kitchen and I heard Ma tell her about my sister who is gone. When Aunty Marta asked what her name had been and Ma told her "Zaha," Aunty broke down sobbing real hard. Ma stayed real quiet and patient, not like her at all, and touched Aunty's arm. Then Aunty Marta said,

"My little Zaha is a Turk now!" and cried some more. Later I asked Pa about it.

"Never you mind that," he said. Sometimes Pa would talk about the old country, like the time he told me about my lost uncle. But it seemed that such times happened less now, and I learned to not ask him questions. If Pa was upset about something, I couldn't bear to be the one in his way, to set him off, God forbid, and break the spell of… of a good day. I waited for him to share words, or not. And for now, what mattered most to him was his sister. He watched when she didn't see, but I did. Like he was worried, I don't know why. For the most part, Aunty Marta seemed happy to be with us and even Ma seemed happy for the company. Everything would have stayed alright, but Uncle Leo came back in March, this time to stay. And all hell broke loose.

Uncle Leo slept on the sofa in the living room with me and Jake. We got to watch him take off his wood leg at night and lay it flat on the floor in front of the sofa where he could reach it in the morning when he woke up, which was always after we got up. One time Jake woke up and wanted to play with the leg. He was fiddling with it when Uncle Leo's arm suddenly shot out of the blanket he was wrapped in, grabbed the leg from Jake and swatted my brother clear across the room with it. Jake let out such a howl, Ma came running. She seldom took the side of us kids when we got in trouble, nor did Pa. Whenever Jake did something wrong, Pa spanked us both. This time, Ma didn't say one word to Jake, while he whimpered in the corner. But she glared at Uncle Leo so hard I expected him to whimper, too. Instead, he just turned over on the sofa like he was going back to sleep, even though it was daytime!

Another time, Susie was toddling around the house, and not bothering anybody. Uncle Leo snatched her by the arm and called out to Ma, "Hey woman, I'll give you a dollar to take this ugly thing down to the lakeshore and drown her!"

After that, I never heard Ma address Uncle Leo directly again. I could tell she hated him. I noticed Pa started sighing a lot and Aunty Marta looked worried. She and Pa spoke together in whispers in that other language. Armenian, Pa called it. And Ma, well, she made no more effort to hide her feelings at all.

I heard her voice in the kitchen when she was fixing lunch with Aunty Marta. "Of course, he showed up after he blew away all his money! And it's not the first time. He never once shared any of his windfall to pay Yussef back for any of our expenses on his behalf." I never heard Aunty Marta say anything back to her. She stayed real quiet about Uncle Leo, and I got the feeling she didn't like to hear Ma complain.

Something else was new. I could hear Ma and Pa arguing from the bedroom at night, though they kept their voices low. Ma's belly was blowing up again and Aunty Marta was going to be married at the end of the year and move away from us.

"The family is growing too big for this farm!" More than a few times I heard her mutter this to Pa. I think I understood Ma. She loved our home and I know she loved us kids. But she didn't love Uncle Leo and I didn't blame her. Maybe Pa didn't either, because he did something about it.

When my birthday came again, this time it was with a big surprise. We were moving. Again! Ma cried and cried; she wailed that she loved our house and farm. She had her brother and her people here, even a priest! She constantly looked out at the lake in the distance and wiped a tear. But all the crying was to the wind, or to me and Aunty. I realized that she didn't let herself cry when Pa was around, but really let it go when he was at work and only we kids were home. Things moved ahead anyway, and she couldn't stop it. Pa finished the planting, even though he said he canceled the lease on the farm. When Ma packed up the house, Uncle Leo left to stay with some men in Detroit. Aunty Marta was already gone to stay with Aunty Mary.

On June 5th, two weeks after my eighth birthday, Pa brought home a real automobile! A touring car, he called it. But then he said, "Now, don't get excited. As soon as we get to Noo York, I sell it, right away."

I didn't care. I tucked my little Model T Ford car inside the pillowcase Ma had stuffed with my clothes. Then I helped her pack up the other clothes, in one pillowcase for each kid. While we were doing this, Ma told me that our life must have some grace from God Almighty because of two things. We were returning to the place where I was born exactly two weeks after my eighth birthday. And, she said, we had left that place exactly two weeks after I was born. Even after we walked to the tree to say goodbye to Zaha, buried under the branches, Ma acted like her mind was changed about moving. She said she was sure this coincidence was a good omen. Pa just laughed at her and shook his head. My body fills with warm sunshine the times they both smile and laugh.

Still, I had some mixed-up feelings when Pa started the car, full of our belongings and all six of us, and rolled down the long gravelly drive away from the house and barn. He stopped halfway down to take a long look at Lake Hune. You could see it so good from our hill. Everyone looked, even Jake and Susie. When I thought about not seeing this big lake again I caught the sadness. At the same time, I was pretty relieved that the feeling in the car was all lightness again; Pa's dimples showed around his mouth from smiling and Ma's eyes gleamed like I hadn't seen for two birthdays. We would miss Aunty Marta's wedding, but Pa said we would be having a nice green summer at Lake *Kay-yoo-gah* and start a new life. He said the wedding would be at the New Year's holiday, too late for us to wait. Funny, that was the last thing I remember hearing before I fell asleep. When I woke up again, the sun was already falling down the sky. Ma laughed at me and said I slept the whole way.

Boy, was I surprised when we pulled up to a little house. Before Ma could stop us, Jake and I jumped out of the car and raced around it, fast as we could. We stopped short at a steep drop-off behind the house and gasped. Our jaws were wide open as we looked at each other, then turned back to look out past it. Stretched out below us was another lake, right in our back yard! This lake was long and narrow. You could see clear to the other shore, and I had the feeling that the other side was not Kanadah. On my left it looked like a line of water that spilled and got blocked by hills at one end. When I turned right and looked forward, the water bent out of sight like a giant worm squiggling to get away. It shimmered and sparkled and seemed to call to me. I ran back to the car where everybody was still climbing out and talking all at once and I asked Pa, "Where do we live now?"

"This is Tubbha," said Ma. "*Kay-oo'ga Lake.*"

"It's Itaka. Itaka, Noo York," Pa said, then sort of whistled through his breath. "Home."

CHAPTER 14

LAND

Port Huron, MI – June 1921

JOE

The idea was hatched where else, but in a shoe shop, of course. For as long as Joe could recall, important ideas and plans were discussed in the shoe shops of his family. Even the Syrian men had begun to frequent Leo's shop, joining the steady stream of Armenians seeking regular conversation in a familiar language. Najeeb had been a firm supporter from the start, out of friendship to Leo, and even his brother, Ameen, stopped by from time to time. Joe supposed that there was a fair amount of awe and trust in anything the Simon brothers did, and it was natural that the Ford crew would follow suit.

Archie and Leo had opened the shop just before the war. But Archie enlisted, serving only six months before he was discharged with tuberculosis. He followed his doctor's advice and headed west to Los Angeles, California. Left with the business, Leo's shop began to thrive when the men trickled back into town at war's end. The numerous boys who had left the Myers salt block for greener pastures at Ford's auto plant, and many more returned from service, took to stretching out a leisurely Sunday afternoon at the shop. That is how Joe learned about farmland back in New York—empty, abandoned acreage being offered for cheap.

"The fields in the hills take the lowest prices, Yussef! It's tougher going for crops, but you can get more land than you can even imagine," cried the young Mahool brother who had just arrived in Detroit. Joe wasn't sure of the boy's name, but his words hit like a brick. He let them simmer for two whole years.

A true farm. As long as he could own fields—not just vegetable patches and fruit trees like the rental in Port Hune, or even back home in Kaladouran—but soil that would sustain a growing family no matter the other income available, even in war time! The idea had sprouted like a seed, but was already popping above the soil of his head in green shoots when he began the long agonizing process of choosing when and how to broach it to Helen.

She was happy on the little patch of land above the big Lake Hune. She had a community of her people and basked in a hostess's place of honor at their gatherings after mass. And she finally enjoyed a blossoming relationship with her brother and his growing family, now settled down on the flats near the salt plant. After meeting his wife, Mary, in Detroit, Moses had followed them to this new place, and seemed content. Mary was popping out boys faster than Helen! What would happen to them, he wondered briefly, if Helen were dragged back out of their lives? Never mind, his concern was with Helen. She would ultimately go along, of course. It was her duty. But an unhappy Helen was a condition no man would choose to live with. She was no meek woman, and he loved her for that. But this would be hard, uprooting her settled existence, especially if she had no choice in the matter. In the end, it was easier than he could have anticipated. All thanks to his brother.

Goddam Leo managed to ruin everything he touched. At the height of the shoe shop traffic, his impulsive brother got an offer he couldn't refuse.

"But Yussef!" Leo took to calling Joe by the Syrian name, never Armenian, nor English. "I can use a break!"

"And for how long will that cash last you, Manas? You gonna give up permanent income for a break?"

There was no swaying Leo when stars got in his eyes. Stubbornness and recklessness would always be his guides. And as usual, Joe was left to pick up the pieces. Sure enough, Leo sold the shop. He ran through his money within two short months and deposited himself on Joe and Helen's sofa. Never lifting a hand to help. Leo had become accustomed to a new way of being in the world: physically helpless because of his leg, yet available to socialize at the drop of a hat with never a hint of the wooden leg behind the folds of his trousers. Helen's face closed down, her lips pinched tighter than Joe had ever seen them. Not even a sigh escaped, as if she couldn't trust herself not to explode if she relaxed her mouth at all. The boys steered clear of Leo, wary if not outright afraid of him. His black moods wafted through the household and the family sunk into silent despair. Nobody dared speak around him or about him.

When Leo inserted himself onto their sofa indefinitely, Joe thought it best to move Marta back to Detroit to wait out her wedding in Mary's household. She was happy with the arrangement. Joe had an ulterior motive. He accompanied Marta to Detroit, then returned on the train the very same day. The sun was lowering and Joe approached Helen in the kitchen where she was beginning supper. He asked her to come to the garden with him, supposedly to hold a grape trellis still while he laced it together. Surely, John or Jake could have been summoned for this simple task. She would instantly realize, he knew, that he needed to talk to her in private.

"Out with it!" she ordered, as soon as she wheeled about in front of him.

"It's about land, Haloun," he began. "Cheap land. In Noo York." He made his case without a word to spare.

She agreed! It surprised him that she did not hold out, or wail, or ask for time, or even openly mourn the loss of her newfound community. He knew she would follow whatever plan he set forth, of course. But if she did not agree, or like it, she would let it be known from the high heavens. In this case, she clearly saw the wisdom for their future. And she likely saw the escape plan. At first her eyes widened. Then she slowly nodded, as solemnly as if she were praying. Her only words: "It is logical." And she grew wistfully excited as they began to prepare.

At times he wondered about her ringed eyes in the early morning. Did she let tears drip into the pillow when she was turned onto her own side? Helen was a force to be reckoned with; she was incapable of withholding what she felt strongly about. Joe decided it best not to interfere with her innermost thoughts. It must be that she agreed with the decision, however much it caused her pain. And so, she would handle it her own way and he would respect her method, just as she clearly respected his responsibility to support the family and his decision making to that end.

Leo was informed and had no option but to head to Detroit. With the typical luck that he enjoyed, and perhaps some good will from past patrons of the shoe shop, he immediately secured accommodation with some single workers at the plants. Joe decided to harvest the early shoots, clean the beds for the next tenant and, hopefully, reach the long finger lakes of New York State by the end of spring.

Ithaca – June, 1921

They spent that summer where they had begun life together. Joe rented one of the eleven little houses on the high cliff of Tubbha (Syrian Hill), overlooking the old salt block that still dominated the lakeshore at Myers. More than a few young Syrian families had flocked to the auto and salt plants in Michigan just as Joe, in stark contrast, brought his young family back. They appreciated the instant benefits that befell them, including the view over the water to the hills rising on the opposite shore, only two miles distant. He hadn't seen Helen so jubilant since just after their wedding, before Leo's accident had inserted its own chaos into their fresh love. She hummed and played with little Nishan (Mitchell) and scolded Jake and Susie less than usual. She reveled in renewed company with old friends and compared notes about the ones who had left for Detroit. The women strolled together amid the clusters of lilac bushes in full bloom on the clearing above the cliff where a church was soon to be built.

This was indeed a lucky piece of the planet for him, he was certain of its rightness. Work, home, and community folded neatly together. In that suspended space and time, Joe acted swiftly with each and any opportunity that presented itself. The first thing Helen had wanted to do was visit their old friends, the Mahools, in Ithaca. After Alice and Abe had a chance to gush over the children, they also went around to see Abe and Anna Abbott. The Abbotts had additional company that day, which is how Joe happened to meet the Syrian owner of the Sideboard Restaurant.

He began work at the restaurant that very week, riding the Lehigh Valley train along the lakeshore between Myers and Ithaca for most of the summer. Those early mornings were precious, when waterfalls roared from even the smallest of side streams that tumbled into the lake, soft green landscapes teased the eyes, and the lake, flat and sleek as smooth glass, stroked Joe's heart. He felt he was witness to the hush that gives birth to each day, before the distractions of life interrupt with riotous purpose.

A few of the men from the restaurant kitchen told Joe about a small farm for sale up the hill south of Ithaca. On his next day off, he decided to take the train back to Ithaca and look at it. It occurred to him that Henna (John) was old enough to accompany him, and he relished the company of his firstborn.

As they walked down the cliff path to the train platform, a few Tubbha men called out to him, again addressing him as Abu Henna. He shot a proud glance at his eight-year-old son. However my children turn out, he thought as the Lehigh Valley train pulled to a stop in front of them, this one will be a rock. The train crept along the lakeshore and Joe settled into his usual reverie, when his son startled him with a question.

"Pa, was the old country like this? Or maybe like Port Hune?" It took Joe some time to think before he formulated an answer. He almost never thought of that life—that place—anymore. In the space of time that he gathered his thoughts, he also made a decision to practice his Amirkan words. He was not certain how much Henna would understand, but it was time to get him on track to be Amirkan.

"Well, Henna, it is like bot places, but different: next to big water, but more big. A sea. Me-di-ter-ra-ne-an. And tese hills around Itaka? Well, Kessab lays across ta bottom part of big mountain called Ak-ra, and more mountains aftuh tat one."

John nodded, as if he had a gift to comprehend deep wisdom, and said no more. Nor did his father. But in the silence that followed the father/son exchange that had, for the first time, not been exclusively in Helen's native Syrian, Joe realized with a jolt, that Henna still had no English. He must get in the school soon, he vowed.

From the Ithaca station they walked a mile through the shopping district, rife with mixed sounds of transportation—car horns, trolley clangs, and horseshoe clinks—reaching the steep incline of South Hill. A half mile up the hill, they saw the sprawling, yellowed structures of a chain plant. On a whim, Joe stopped and inquired about work. Quite surprisingly, a foreman took his application. Even more fortunate, since he could not have done so himself, the foreman took it upon himself to ask the questions and fill out the form, writing out Joe's name, age, and experience at salt blocks and Ford Co. It seemed there was an opening for a machinist to work the boilers, so that day was Joe's lucky day, even more so that the man was none the wiser that Joe could not write the information for himself. Father and son trudged another mile up the steep hill, often glancing behind them at a breathtaking view of Cayuga Lake and the surrounding hills that embraced it.

The available farmland, twenty-five acres in total, began just beyond the intersection of King Road and Danby, east to the crest of the hill, and then "a little more," as had been described to Joe. At the top of the long rise to the crest stood a small, green-shingled house and modest barn. Farther down the other side, he could see several farmhouses and it was easy to guess where the property boundaries stood. The house was nestled among potato fields and groves of unkempt berry bushes that made an abrupt decline past the shrub line, beyond which stretched the pasturelands of downhill farms.

All in one day, a job was secured, a home and acreage discovered, and father and son arrived home in jubilant exhaustion. Over the past few years, Joe had managed to support his family with the Port Huron salt plant salary, and still put away meager profits from farming and moonshining the Arak whiskey he made from a copper still, always kept hidden from view in the basement. The savings was just barely enough. Within a week the farm was negotiated and purchased with his

$800, the move planned for summer's end. With elated hearts, the Joe Peter family enjoyed the annual fireworks display over Myers Point on the Fourth of July. They packed baskets, strolled down the steep slope from Tubbha with the Abrahams, Georges, and Solomons, and joined the entire Syrian community on the park grounds along the Salmon River inlet.

When the color bursts that broke the blackness of the night matched the excitement in his children, Joe thought about his last summer days of boyhood on the Kaladouran beach. There are no loose ends remaining there, he thought, two sisters and two brothers were now safe in Amirka. He said a little prayer for Hayrig, Mayrig, and Nishan in the old country, for his own little ones, Jirgis and Zaha, and allowed himself a brief minute to wonder about brother Asadour—in Brazil, perhaps. He then shifted his thoughts to cousin Asadour with a bottomless gratitude for his cousin's devotion to family that had helped reunite him with his sisters. Hopefully, Asadour and his beloved Louisa would soon join them on this soil. What could be done was done, and in that thought lived contentment. His heart was full and ready when the last sparks floated to the water, the last boom faded into the night, and the gentle slap of lapping waves, again audible, caressed his ears.

At the end of the first summer back in New York, the family moved into the little green house on King Road. Helen managed the potato field, the meals, and the younger children. Joe worked his shift, planted vegetables, and again saved a little each week from peddling produce and milk. He sometimes could even spare a bit of cash for card games with the Italian men from work, to some of whom he sold produce.

In September, Joe walked down the hill to the corner where King and Danby Roads collided. There stood a single room, clapboard building on the corner. The schoolhouse. He arranged for John to enter 2nd grade and Jake to enter 1st grade. He also made an agreement with a woman across the street to provide the children with a meal for lunch. His eight- and six-year-old sons were about to confront life in English. And then the hard part. He would tell Helen, Susie would go in the next year.

"Why on earth…?" she would cry. He did not expect her to understand and knew she would balk about sending a girl to school, an idea that was *odar* to her.

In the old country, only Armenian girls got the school, thought Joe. It is something important that Arabs missed in life. He didn't know why this was. He only knew that his kids would get everything Amirka had to offer, especially education. It was time.

The walk to Morse Chain Company was an easy stride downhill, first on King Road, and the remaining two miles on Danby Road. It was a good deal more strenuous on the way back home after a tiring shift. Occasionally, one of two Finnish farmers whose farms bordered Joe's would pass by and offer a lift. Regardless, the beauty of the walk downhill made the return up South Hill well worth the effort. The rolling hills that hugged the bottom end of Cayuga Lake and Ithaca always spoke to Joe in ways like no place he had known in Michigan.

Since the day he stepped off the wrong train onto the Ithaca platform, some fifteen years earlier, the gently sloping landscape here had brushed against his bones. He knew now, that he belonged to it. Something about the wooded hills, deep-cut gorges, and sprawling snake-like bodies of water squirming amongst them—though unlike the arid gorges and mountainside slopes of Kessab—engaged him physically at the deepest place and evoked a calming wonder. Although the climate resembled that of Michigan, crunching over the pristine white snow in these silent, sacred spaces rendered the cold season more tolerable than trudging among the factories and plants that lined the shores of the St. Claire River while under attack from blistering winds that sliced through bone. When the winter's grey and blustery days would finally pass, Joe never failed to whistle out loud while walking down Danby Road toward the plant, the full view of Cayuga Lake confronting him from a near distance. Between both shores of the lake, close together and gloriously green under a cobalt sky, the lake's water itself stretched away to the north and bent out of sight at the very spot where Myers Point jutted out into the water from the east shoreline. He thought about how many times he had stood on that point in his first years in Amirka, his eyes seeking out Helen's.

CHAPTER 15

BIRTHING
Ithaca, NY - October 1921

HELEN

In New York's Finger Lakes region, the colors of October often reach their peak on the third weekend of the month, later than in New England, the Adirondacks, or even the hills that crowd close together south of Ithaca. Unless a strong wind or hail has dislodged the leaves from their home branches by that time, one may revel in, almost worship, the miracle of this triumph of Mother Nature. The low-hanging clouds may well have morphed into a brilliant, crystalline sky, considering the brightness given off by oranges, golds, and reds that surrounded and lit the air with a dizziness that nature seldom produced for Helen. She did not know the word "peak." Her version of the color bubble that enveloped her, as she dug potatoes on the 21st day of October, would be earthier in either language of her world—Syrian or English.

Ripe, just like me, she thought as she straightened her burdened body, placing her hand on her arched back to stretch out the kink. The wave of the first contraction attacked with hurricane force; like a gust, filled up the unnatural curve in her backside and blew her backward a step.

"Eeeyaai!" she let out a hiss and, in the same moment, mentally identified the exact spot where three-year-old Susie was cuddling and cooing at the baby, Mitch. Ah there, in the yard where she could see them, of course. Calculations filled her mind—the same mind that lacked the training to read but could always figure out exactly how much money her husband may have lost at cards to his Italian friends on Friday nights. Her assessment now was that it was best to forego topping off the potato basket and instead gather the little ones inside before the contractions came on too fast. As it was, she needed to clean up before the birth came, to keep everything as simple as possible until the moment when she could not control anything outside of her own racking body.

The space of minutes between contractions sped up immediately. She knew the score. This was her seventh time at full delivery; she did not count two additional miscarriages. With brisk steps, she swooped Nishan onto her hip with a painful grunt and herded Susie into the house with the promise of a mission. Susie was too small to carry an eleven-month baby, but she was able to enjoy a serious role, to play and keep the baby near her. Helen guessed he was due for his afternoon sleep anyway. She dumped the basket of potatoes by the basin, pumped water into her largest pot, boiled the water on the stove, hauled Mitch, towels, and knife upstairs, and set Susie and the baby down in the bedroom doorway to "stand watch."

It was not a moment too soon. A groan escaped her lips as the contraction launched her onto the bed. From the corner of her eye, she saw Susie's head shoot up in alarm and thought, she may as well learn sooner than later. Nothing else for a girl.

Her next thought flew to dear Zahea—Flora—Abraham, who had been there to guide her through the first birth, of little Henna, just two weeks before the trek to Michigan. For the others, there had always been someone who came to her from the communities of Highland Park and Port Hune. Should she be frightened now? Mercifully, she had no more time to think or hesitate.

It hardly felt like pushing. Less than ten minutes later, her second Jirgis, whom the kids would call George, practically slid out like he hadn't a care waiting for him in the world, and no more need for her dark womb. Or, perhaps the tunnels from her womb were so stretched that there was little pain to feel. Either way, a blessing, praise be to God and the mother Mary! And may God grant all future births to be this easy. That is, if she must have more. And if so, may the next one be a girl—and the last.

George's infant cry sliced right into her prayers and brought Susie toddling to her bedside. Mitch had fallen asleep in the hall. She reached for the knife she had placed beside the bed and, with Jirgis tucked into a towel, she pulled herself up far enough to grab ahold of the cord and slice through it in two places. Then she cooed to her three-year-old daughter, now studying the baby with wonder, to hold onto the baby's side so he couldn't roll off the bed while Helen took a deep breath and pushed out the afterbirth, also easy this time. Now, conscious to keep the gooey liquid hidden from her child's view, she swooped it into a second towel and wrapped it tightly. Carrying both bundles, she pulled herself from the bed and stumbled down the stairs to the kitchen, calculating how much time before the newborn would discover his first earthly sensation—of hunger.

Helen tucked George into Mitch's hearth cradle, a wood and wicker rocking affair that no child in this household had occupied for more than a year. There had been a birth almost every year since she became Helen Peter. Susie sat herself down beside the cradle, still gazing adoringly, and began to rock the new "doll." She'd been only two when Mitch was born, not having developed this instinct; only now, did doll play seed in her child's mind. Helen slipped out the back door, quickly buried the afterbirth, stepped back into the kitchen, washed her hands, retrieved the big pot upstairs, washed herself, washed little Jirgis in the cradle, and rewrapped him in a fresh towel. Then she picked up the basket she'd left by the basin, put the pot to boil, and peeled at least a dozen potatoes before John and Jake burst into the house. They looked like they had run all the way up the King road from the schoolhouse at the Danby Road intersection. She laughed to think they may have sensed they had a new baby at home. They ran over to the cradle for a peek, then ran outside for chores before supper.

While she cooked potatoes with a little lamb meat and the last of the greens of the season, Helen made a note to herself: May this child honor the one of his name who came before. May 'Jirgis the First' rest in peace with knowledge of his namesake, born the day of his burial, seven years now past.

It felt like a formality, these words in her mind, a private ritual completed. But then she had another thought that made her laugh: And I must remember to tell the new child how easily he chose to enter the world.

CHAPTER 16

COMMUNITY

Ithaca - February 1923

JOE

Six children and counting, thought Joe. In October, Helen had given birth to yet another boy and named him Samuel. Over the dark winter months, when he normally lingered in the warmth of her body for longer than usual, she joked that she needed a break. It took him by surprise. In his confusion, his thoughts wandered aimlessly to his own childhood. They had been seven children altogether, so he smiled, wondering if he might reach that number as well, and if his mother might be looking on proudly. Rich, rich, rich, that's what I am! he thought to himself, even if no more. Six children is a fortune!

Then, he remembered. The seventh child had taken his mother's life. Joe leaped out of the bed to find a chore to do fast enough to push the thought away. He was too happy to allow it space. Helen stirred and raised her head to watch him, then sank back on the pillow, too tired to follow. When he looked back at her form under the blanket, he swelled with the wonder of his life. He could care for these treasures, he would do anything for them. Plenty of ways to make life work.

When spring came, he took the two oldest boys with him and walked down the hill, then turned west to the flats below. When they asked where they were headed, he just winked and said, "It's a surprise."

The building, crouched on the wetlands below South Hill, had just one story, and was built from stone. It was part house and part store, with a lot of automobiles parked outside. Joe pointed to one of the vehicles and told John and Jake to wait for him in that car while he went inside. They looked at him incredulously. Joe chuckled to himself, knowing that they had never been in a car with no roof! Or rather, there was a sort of cloth roof folded at the back and once they walked around the vehicle and studied it, well, he could see them work out that it must be a roof that opens and closes. They had not even been in a car since the journey from Port Hune to Myers. He had bought that short-lived vehicle to serve one purpose, move the family, and sold it immediately upon their arrival, before work was secured to support his family. Now, his sons climbed into the front seat and beamed with pride, dreaming perhaps that somebody they knew would chance by and see them.

After a while, Joe emerged from the doorway, followed by a taller man who had to bend down to duck through the frame. Joe turned and shook hands with the man who clapped him on the back, then strolled right over to the car and, motioning for the boys to hop in back, climbed into the driver seat. The man climbed in the other side, showed Joe some pointers about operating the car, then got out and waved them off.

"Think you can handle it, Joe?" he called.

"I tink so, tank you. Goot bye." Joe's clipped English was brief and concise. The boys went wild with whoops and hollers as Joe started that car right up and drove it away from that place, taking them for a ride around the flats in the 1916 Chevy Touring Car before they headed back up South Hill to home.

But when winter arrived, he determined the cloth top to be less than optimal. Before the New Year, Joe traded in the Touring Car for a brand-new Maxwell and, on the first Sunday in spring, he herded Helen and all six kids into the car and drove them to Tubbha, or Syrian Hill, at Myers. A brand-new Orthodox Church had been built on the cliff clearing, just for the Syrians who lived there and worked at the salt plant. Mass ended at noon and the grand opening festivities began. Food included shishkabob, numerous platters of pilaf, taboule, shadiyeh, loobee, and all manner of vegetables, such as cabbage and squash, stuffed with ground lamb, onions, and peppers. Joe brought his own baked round loaves of bread. Olives and yogurt graced every table set up on the sweeping lawn that overlooked the lake and Myers Park below. Someone played the oud and another man's fingers flew across the stretched goat skin of a dumbek, a familiar rhythm pattern that reached all the way to Joe's groin, prompting a dozen or so men up from their chairs, some reaching for their handkerchiefs to accompany the stamping feet.

Joe turned his gaze to Helen. He loved to study her while she watched her boys race around, check that Susie and Mitch were sitting with a circle of children and, only then, allow herself a wistful glance at the park below, where they had married and enjoyed so many Sundays and July holidays. He knew the cliff, on which Tubbha perched above the lake, reminded her of the plateau where her hometown of Melkia overlooked the Mediterranean Sea in the old country. He also knew that the air caressing her face was different here and represented a gentler life. He suspected she might just be thinking about that as he watched her sigh with contentment, then rise to join the line of women dancing the debke.

CHAPTER 17

GAMAVOR

Kaladouran - 1923

LOUISA

Asadour entered the kitchen with such a heavy trod, I looked up in alarm. It was late in the day, even for the Gamavor facing skirmishes on the mountain slopes above Kessab center. And he had been at it for most of the day, taking a shift that began before noon. Typically, the regular attacks from rogue Turks had fallen into the daily pattern of early morning hours and again at dusk. Most of the men from the village were in the rotation, guarding the perimeter around all of Kessab from aggressors. Asadour closed the shoe shop on the days of his duty.

Now, his face said it all, though it seldom lit up these days. Ever since the boys...

"We will never be safe, Louisa. I am in despair."

"You boys have been able to repel them for going on five years already. What makes your confidence run away now?" It was not my intention to sound cynical; and I regretted the choice of words which might seem so. I truly was surprised—alarmed—at his mood. Perhaps he has lost his will, his reason, I thought, without our boys to live and fight for.

"Ataturk has taken power. The French have snuck away, I cannot bring myself to believe it. Armenia is lost, Cilicia is again a dangerous home for all, even more so now that we have fought. Fought and won, God damn it! And for what?!"

Then my husband slumped onto the chair closest to the door, lowered his head, and wept into his arms. I held my instinct to rush to him in check. It was good, this cleansing. He wept for his country. He wept for his parents, his sisters and brothers. Finally. And most of all, he wept for our two sons.

The birth of Khatchig and then, within the year, Giragos— one right after the other— had cracked the world open in Kaladouran. The war-weary villagers who had survived to return home burst alive, as did we, with the arrival of innocent children, unencumbered by our recent experiences. The boys inserted themselves into this small world above the sea with such innocence, oblivious to the heaviness that the rest of us dragged around, and with fresh delight in each new discovery of the world around them: the ripening of grapes on the vines, the messiness of pomegranate seeds, the mustaches of the men. The witnessing of such curiosity infused each inhabitant of Kaladouran with light that appeared in the brown and grey pupils of their eyes and spread to the spring in their step. The eldest giggled out loud whenever the boys toddled by laughing, tripping, and often pointing at some insect or other creature resting in the palm of a hand.

How can such joy lead to such pain? Did I do something to bring on the demise of my children? Did I fail to care for myself and pass on a disease for which they were no match? They called it typhoid. Many suffered it in the camps. But after all that I survived, how could I not save them? Have I let down the entire village? My husband? It is inevitable to follow these thoughts, because no explanation is available.

My guilt stops me short at times, when I am near Shoushan, who lost her girl. Frieda, her first born—died in Jordan, in the camp. And the baby… but losing children in those circumstances is possible, or so I tell myself. This is not. Our safe return, to Asadour's childhood home, our redemption. How is it possible to bring forth God's greatest gift, not once, but twice, only to lose his gifts? God. He took them back. The loss to Asadour drives a knife into my fresh wounds, doubles the pain, now and every day. It does not relent.

I almost told him. Right then. But it is not time. He needs to have his grief first. Besides, I am not entirely sure…

The next morning, we walked together to Kessab; Asadour to the shoe shop and I to the school. It had been almost four months since I was with the students, not since the boys took ill nor since they lost the battle, first Giragos, then Khatchig. My heart—I could not fathom what I felt; my feelings were still so jumbled. I could not make out what I wanted or needed. Except that I was ready for numbness to be over. Being at the school would either ease or intensify my pain. There was no way to guess which, I thought, so I may as well throw myself at the task. We walked in silence, but it was not a fraught silence. I sensed that Asadour had calmed. Almost like when he has a purpose, it suddenly occurred to me. I had seen that in him, during the war, and after…. carving out a new life in the face of emptiness. I imagined no such mission at this point, yet I was relieved that yesterday's anguish was diminished. We arrived at the shop door. There stood his cousin, Khatchig, waving a letter.

"Elisa is coming! She wrote that she has left Antioch already. I must drive a cart to Aleppo and see if she is on the train. I cannot imagine how else she will find her way to Kessab." He rushed out the words and raced off just as hurriedly, leaving us no time to reply. We watched his back as he strode downhill to the stable, then looked at one another, mouths agape.

Elisa, home. I pictured the child I had taught, so young when she was taken. Inside all the fear she must have endured, somehow she had created purpose. Her studies had saved her. I knew this based on her decision to stay four years ago, when we wrote to fetch her. When Ataturk had come to power and most Armenians in Turkey were being sent to Greece for safety, Elisa wrote again that she had six months more to complete. Elisa was last studying in Antioch. Evidently, it was no longer safe for her to remain there.

Perhaps this is a blessing that Kessab needs. Another teacher! This was actually the first thought that came to me, and I felt no shame for it. Elisa wanted to teach. Our community was in need. Something had fallen into place, at last. Something was as it should be. I couldn't wait.

Gradually, I realized that I was looking forward to something. It was the first positive emotion I had felt in many days, weeks, months. And I knew I would tell Asadour that night. Perhaps a new corner was upon us. I almost smiled as I turned to walk on to the school. At least I knew I was ready to face my students. Elisa's arrival would soon change everything.

All day long, I gazed at the students and yearned for my boys. But I also cherished the moments with the children in class. In the afternoon, we walked a ways up the slopes of Jabal Aqra for fresh air and singing. All the boys and girls loved the breaks on the mountain. Even the boys sang, buoyed by the breeze and sensation of being on top of the world, overlooking red and blue rooftops sprawled below us. We could see the domes of the Apostelic Church and the Catholic one amidst the houses of Kessab, some occupied once more, though most remained empty.

The steeple of the Evangelical Church was attached to our mission school, which had closed for too long, but reopened when two missionaries returned to Kessab. There were few students now. So many did not survive the march or the camps. I pictured Elisa before the war, flush with the discovery of learning. I said a silent prayer of gratitude for her return, to share the love she has found in studies.

The journey from Aleppo could not be done in a day, and so we did not stop at Khatchig's home before we returned to the village that night. Nor did I manage to contain my news until we arrived at home. Instead, when we reached the rise at Karadash, where the path levels and all of the valley below unfolds before our eyes from where we stand there, on Jabal Dapusa, I sucked in a long drink of the thin air and knew I would explode.

"My love, Asadour-jan, do you suppose we can handle a bit of happiness at last?"

He looked at me quizzically, with patience, yet also with the innocence of a lack of imagination one finds oneself stuck in when numbness has set in for long enough to dull the senses. I chose to savor the moment, that space in time that hovers between knowing and not knowing something that may change one's life. I enjoyed his waiting and felt the impact of it spread across my face like a flush of lightness. He deserved this. We deserved it. I prayed he was ready to receive my gift, our redemption.

"I am not completely certain, but I missed something while caring for the boys, when we were fighting to save them, when I wasn't paying attention…" The fact that his face hadn't changed was shocking. That he could be so void of understanding, unable to guess… suddenly, I chuckled. I was mentally blaming him for the very same cluelessness I was describing of myself!

"Asadour, I am with… we are with child. Maybe four, five months already!"

It was so slow, the dawning of understanding, his taking in the words. Words he never expected. Slow, but worthwhile. The grin came so slowly, it was like watching a painter create a face, moving one muscle at a time, shades changing as the face is invaded by comprehension. And finally, the face completely lit in beaming rays, his joy fully visible. As the transformation took place, the sun in the sky had also been maneuvering to the exact position that embraced us in floodlit reds and golds. It was a moment of grace, a blessing and undeniable symbol from forces beyond our ability to conceive. My love and I would again know joy and redemption. We were chosen for it.

Manase was born in November. The 15th day. Shoushan was there for me. And Elisa took on my students. Her training with me was more important than anyone could have imagined, and just in time. I could not walk to Kessab for several weeks, nor leave Manase without milk for more than two hours at a time.

Asadour returned to the shoe shop, though he had taken to closing at times to fish, even on the days he was not on duty with the freedom fighters, the Gamavor. There was not much business in new shoes from destitute neighbors, and we were mighty fortunate for the garden that sustained us. Asadour was beginning to fret that the shop would not carry us for long.

Yet peace was returning to his heart. My husband and I had seen much death during the war. I believe that like most survivors, we had a special ability to crawl from our depth of sorrow and dive into living. We lost our families. But we found one another. Then we lost the family we made for ourselves. Now we saw our second chance to reclaim life.

This caused Asadour to think hard again about Amirka. He talked of his work there. He had lived in three places: Noo York, Weesconsin, Deetroyt. Always, there was work, he said. Boghos and Asadour both held the dream to take their brides back to Amirka. Asadour now went to Ladehkiya to discuss emigration with the missionaries, to learn of the process, and to speak with the Red Cross officials who had helped us send Marta to her brothers. Asadour returned distraught.

We now learned that not long after Marta had gone, the door to the new world had already closed on us. The United States decided to stop the flow of emigrants from our part of the world after the war had coughed so many to its shores. Amirka had grown weary of its swelling masses of *odar* faces.

"We waited too long," said Asadour. My heart broke for my husband, who had been so certain of a future there.

CHAPTER 18

NEWS

Ithaca - 1925

HELEN

Helen knew what a telegram was, of course. But never had she been delivered one. After a few hours, the shock faded into a perpetual nervousness, and she made a determined decision to calm herself. She ticked off in her head, in a mathematical way, a list of possible relatives far from their little New York farm. Only Mary or Martha had occasionally written letters to Yussef, and this was not a normal letter. Perhaps it was from Asadour, in Syria? She knew her own parents to be dead. Cousins Abe and Martha had brought the news when they settled in Geneva, over on Seneca Lake. She supposed her only sister was still in Syria. But she could not write, nor could her brother Moses, so it must be from Yussef's family. Still, she was uneasy. A telegram can come from anywhere. Please, God, let it not be bad news!

Helen missed her brother now. Once he had married in Detroit, and then settled in Port Hune, she grew accustomed to having him in her daily life. She regretted that raising their kids together was no longer something she could look forward to. She had recently heard, through Melkia folks traveling to and from Michigan, that Moses had lost the job at the salt plant and headed to Detroit to look for work. That must be hard for Mary and the children, Helen now thought, stuck in the little flat near the plant in Port Huron. Mose had always needed more than luck and his own tenacity—he typically required a bit of help and connections—so she said a little prayer for him. It is strange how minds often flow in the direction where they are most needed. Helen had more skill than this: she had, in fact, developed a belief in her own premonitions, often dreaming of events before they happened or suffering from visions portending things she preferred not to be aware of. So she was completely taken off guard, clueless, on the December day that the telegram arrived.

All day long Helen glanced at it lying on the side table and anguished while she waited for Yussef to return from work. By now, all the children were in school except George and Sam. The two of them, four- and three-years-old respectively, tended to entertain each other for hours, leaving enough open space for her tortured imagination to simmer unchecked. Despite a miscarriage the prior year, and a good deal of pain for months after, Helen's belly was again swollen to the point that she suspected only a few months remained. Hormones and anxiety compounded to threaten the typical grounding by which she walked through her days, and were out of her control by the time John, Jake, Mitch, and Susie burst into the house. She snapped sharply at them to come help her dig potatoes, desperate as she pulled and yanked and cursed at the potatoes, tossing them in her basket as if they were guilty of enormous sins.

When Joe turned off the car ignition, Helen and every one of his children flew at him, all containing a nervousness for which they had no understanding. They crowded about him, making it difficult to move, and all talked at once, but it was Helen's voice that cut through.

"A telegram, Yussef! What can it be?" she wailed, grabbing the envelope and slapping it into his hands. He slowly removed the folded sheet from the envelope, then looked back up, embarrassed, and turned to John.

"It's in English…. you read?"

John took the paper, proud of his new reading skills, and sounded out the words with seriousness. "Moses dead STOP Streetcar ak-sident STOP Please help STOP Mary."

Detroit, Ithaca - 1925

JOE

For two days, Helen was inconsolable. She muttered to herself, to her hands, to the pots she washed, to the potatoes, to the youngest kids as she dressed them, to God especially.

"That poor woman! Those poor boys! Dear God! That poor woman!" she repeated incessantly. She cried, too, not caring who witnessed.

Joe had not known this kind of despair in his wife since Zaha had died. He ached inside to see her pain. Three days after the telegram arrived, Joe returned from work and told her, "My boss said take four days to go. Go get them…" Helen instantly burst into tears, her relief and love for her husband keenly felt by Joe. She had not asked. He had not said anything to her. But she did not know that he had spent the past two days obsessed with little else at work, in the barn, milking the cow.

Thoughts appeared in an orderly pattern: my wife has been gracious to each of my sisters and attended to them lovingly in their need. She has suffered my brother's rage and poor behavior. More than once. This is family. Who else but us to take them in?

All that had remained was to know if he would risk his job for what he knew he must do. Now, with risk removed, the decision felt light, unencumbered.

"I'll bring them. Then we find them help."

Joe drove straight to Detroit, driving through the blind night. In the morning, he breakfasted at Marta's house and allowed himself some moments to enjoy his two sisters as they fluttered about and fussed over him. He then purchased a casket, and collected the body from the city morgue where two kind employees helped him secure the casket to the top of the car. Without hesitation, he pointed the car and casket toward Port Huron, to collect Moses' widow Mary, her five boys, and baby girl. They barely fit: eight bodies squeezed into the car, all belongings stuffed in the small trunk, and casket strapped to the hood. It was deep into December. The roads were treacherous with drifting snow and Joe clenched the steering wheel with more apprehension than his usual fearless approach to weather and basic challenges. These souls, so dependent on him, were suspended in unknown territory. They had no vision of future, could not comprehend their present and, surely, had nothing to cling to, except hope and trust in him in the moment. He shuddered with the enormous weight of it, and silently prayed he could always provide for his own family.

Once home, he arranged for a funeral at the new church on Syrian Hill, and a burial in the cemetery nearby, in spite of the snow-covered ground. One by one, the Syrians paid their respects to the deceased. Mary and Helen sat solemnly together against a wall, receiving a stream of sympathies and tears from the women of Tubbha. The men from Melkia, who had once sworn themselves his enemy, now respectfully clapped him on the back, in awe of Joe's character and charity. They referred to him in a variety of ways: Yussef, Bete, and Abu Henna. Only the few Americans present called him Joe.

Moses' five boys may have been in shock, or some form of grief; most of them reacted with various forms of awkwardness, such as grunts and snickers, to the attention heaved upon them by virtual strangers. Joe thought to himself that the boys might harbor some amount of distrust toward 'the man who was taking over their lives.' Joe noticed his John flinch when they addressed him as 'Bete'—the name they overheard the other Syrian men call Joe—rather than 'Uncle.' The term infuriated their cousin, who seemed to consider it disrespectful to his father. But the Moses boys, floundering in the surreal situation they discovered themselves in, could have little grasp of behavior or expectation. Life had instantly run away from them, and Joe sensed there was no sorting out the unfamiliar feelings flying through their hearts and minds. He recognized something in the silent faces of his nephews: helplessness. It sparked a memory.... an overnight transition to a motherless home and, later, losing all his world in one day—home, family, country, language. Joe shook it off with a long shudder and turned to assess his newly inflated household.

Life on King Road altered the instant the carload of cousins piled out of the Maxwell. Only John, who expected some form of gratitude from his shell-shocked cousins, harbored any tension, a resentment based on certain unrealistic expectations of an eldest child, who was not allowed to project such attitude onto his own siblings and dared not reveal his feelings toward these cousins to his parents. But the altered world of the Peter household was naturally exciting for the younger boys, elated by the gift of new playmates.

Joe and Helen, determined to embrace Moses' family and to help them heal, plunged head first into practical challenges. Cots were purchased and borrowed and set up in the two large bedrooms upstairs. The new dormitories were divided between the older boys with John Peter, Moses Jr., Jake, John Mose, and George Mose, in one room. Another room held the younger boys: Frank, Mitch, Nicholas, George Peter, and Sam. Susie slept with her Aunt Mary and Mary's baby, also named Susan. Space was tight, but doable. Words were unspoken. But the sounds of boys and daily tasks filled the rooms and the days.

CHAPTER 19

BOYS
Ithaca - 1926

HELEN

The younger kids were resilient and got along fine. Helen took special note of eight-year-old George Moses, who took four-year-old George Peter under his wing, allowing the littler 'Jirgis' to follow him everywhere without complaint. The older boys teamed up by age and chores: every child had assignments to do his or her part on the farm. But the year felt long and fraught with obstacles, and the two families co-existed without serious bonding. Helen struggled to be as cheerful possible, though inwardly worried about her sister-in-law. She had never known Mary intimately enough in Port Huron to have a clue how to help her now. And when her own time came, she had already surmised that poor Mary was also pregnant!

Like Helen, Mary had stepped off a boat into a new world, a teenaged girl following a brother into the unknown. Mary had arrived at the Port of Detroit via Canada. Introduced and married to Moses Mike at twenty, her babies started coming just one year after Helen's first. Perhaps, because Mary had not stood out in any individual way at Moses' side, Helen could not imagine Mary managing on her own and did not, at first, see her as capable. She made a serious effort to befriend her now. With two women and two families inhabiting one space, naturally, the single kitchen presented every opportunity for connection.

"Will you make the shadiyeh today, Mary? I need to bring in the last of the potatoes before the frost. It will be too dark for the kids to help after school." A tenuous beginning.

Like the other sister-in-law named Mary, this Mary said little in return. And Helen was able to identify an acute pity for this woman, a more natural compassion than she had been able to muster over a decade earlier for that other, mysterious, proud and foreign Mary, whose tribulations could not be accessed out loud and only lurked in the recess of everyone's imagination. But though Helen could feel for Mary Moses on a deeper level, it was not without some little dread, knowing that her own responsibilities would not soon fade away.

That Christmas, a dark stormy sixth day of January, the icy roads were too dangerous to attend the church in Myers. It was inconceivable to create and provide a gift for each of the many children in the household. The two families played games and created as best a feast as they could manage. The household woke to the aroma of baking bread, courtesy of Joe. Hot chocolate was made for breakfast. Helen watched as the Peter boys solemnly demonstrated to their cousins its purpose for the dunking of rolled up pieces of their father's piping hot Syrian bread. For her nephews' sakes, Helen told stories throughout the day of the village named Melkia, Syria, where she and their father had grown up. Riveted, they all whistled at the description of Helen's father, also named Moses, stealing his own donkey back from the Muslim man who had stolen it from him. They gasped at how their grandfather, who was known as Abu Haloun (father of Helen), often placed her in a tree to hide her until certain riders had passed safely out of sight, so she, too, wouldn't be stolen. They giggled—Jake Peter and his cousin Moses even snickered—to learn how garlic was stuffed into the cracks of stone walls to discourage snakes from entering the houses. When she got ready to tell the funniest part of a tale, she would begin laughing so hard she lost the ability to speak and could only choke it out in spurts and squeals. Her audience of twelve rapt faces had to wait an interminable length of time to hear the story's end. Helen's children would later learn to ask for the least funny stories when they gathered evenings around the stove, the ritual that became their primary form of entertainment on winter nights, in the hope of hearing a story through to its end, uninterrupted. But Helen would just laugh and tell whatever came to her mind, anyway.

On a blizzardy morning in February, Helen delivered another boy. This one she named for her late brother, Moses. It was comforting, for the first time in her married life, to have another woman on hand to help in this fraught and challenging time. She was able to remain in bed for most of the day, content that the wood for the stove would not run out and that the youngest of her children were well looked after. Even supper was not of her concern, so she relaxed in bed with the newborn suckling her breast and marveled at the luxury. Now that her infant was safely snuggled in her arms, it was time to address the thing that was clear to her. Her brother's wife entered the room with a cup of tea. She leaned to place Helen's only fine set of cup and saucer on the bedside stand, and straightened with a touch of hesitancy to which only Helen would have noticed and assigned any significance.

"Can you feel you are with child, Mary? I am certain of it!"

"I suppose it is true. And I hope for a girl, who I can name Helen." The sisters-in-law beamed at one another, as Mary gathered up the infant and exited the room so that Helen might sleep a bit more.

EPILOGUE

Lost and Found

Ithaca - 2021

Author

My two personal heroes did finally get to meet. In the 1980s, my parents took a train tour west across the United States to southern California, where they were warmly welcomed into the home of Stepan and Seta Karamardian. No one could have guessed it was a visit not to be repeated, due to Stepan's untimely death less than a decade later. I was reminded of it recently while combing through a bin of parental paperwork, which contained letters I had sent them in 1977, bursting with the excitement of discovering the California clan of Karamardians. One of these begged a missive of my Dad.

"Dad, can you please write your memories of growing up on the South Danby farm? And interview the Detroit family—reach your aunts while they still live—get their stories, while I search for Jido's?" He enthusiastically agreed.

One of the obscurities that always plagued me was the question of my great aunts living in Detroit. The first story about them that either I recalled, or imagined, was that their brothers had bought them out of Turkish harems and brought them to America! Once I met Stepan, I tried to shelve the curiosity about their lives until Louisa's diary, once translated to English, would provide the true details. Yet, the Detroit thing continued to gnaw at me. That they would bring the sisters all the way to the United States, only to live halfway across the country from any of them. When I grew up, my Jido (Joe) lived with us in New York State and both Archie (Khatchig) and Leo (Manas) were living in Los Angeles. I had no idea that all three brothers had been living in Michigan at the time that first Mary, and then Martha, came to the new country, with the great war occurring between their arrivals! All these years we had been throwing around stories based on the vaguest of information. By this time, Mary had died, but Dad did receive a letter from Martha and her daughter describing the ordeal when the Turks came and took her away. He also collected accounts from the aunts whom we called Big Alice and Little Alice, both first cousins of my grandfather and who lived near Mary and Martha and shared their Detroit lives. Big Alice (Chalakian) was an Injejikian by birth; Little Alice (Margossian) was a Karamardian, who shared her story of kidnapping, orphanages, and a quest for education.

My Uncle John, whom I interviewed for a decade throughout his nineties, had an uncanny access to long-term memory. Reaching back to his childhood, he described the aunties who came from the old country and stayed with them. His impressions offered a cinematic glimpse into the Michigan years of the family and filled in gaps I didn't know existed.

"The old man was restless; he moved us around and back and forth! Detroit, Port Huron, Detroit, Flint, back to Port Huron…" He especially recalled a farm at Port Huron.

"We could see the lake from our house on a hill…"

He even remembered street addresses. He shared conversations and memories of visitors, of attitudes—those of his mother strongly influenced him—toward people Jido cared for and helped. John shared many specific feelings he had witnessed from his mother, such as those toward Leo, her brother-in-law. He outlived all his younger brothers, until just a few weeks shy of his one hundredth birthday. Many of these perceptions were confirmed by my aunts, but they could not offer much insight into the soul of Joe Peter, the silent parent.

John, as the eldest, had worked with his father from the age of fourteen. As far as I can tell, he was the only person to whom Joe Peter shared tidbits of information about his travels to America and his time spent in the islands, peddling, baking, making friends with locals. The family's return to Ithaca and farm life was not questioned by eight-year-old John, when Joe Peter had dreamed again and rearranged his physical environment. (And so, it seems, had rearranged mine!)

My father's excitement at meeting the face of Bedros Karamardian was matched by a discovery of my own. I came across a folded newspaper in Dad's musty files. It was an issue of the Armenian Reporter from August 16, 1984. I do not know if he was aware of what it meant, but at first, it threw me off track.

I was still wrapped up in the mystery of Asadour, the lost brother, who disappeared to South America and had not been heard from again. But with so many miscommunications, missed clues about family whereabouts, it was natural that I could be easily distracted by the common names I would come across. The folded section of the weekly Armenian paper from August 16, 1984 was about "The Armenian Legionnaires Memorial Program." It included an expanded roster that had been revised from "a comprehensive listing of 1,172 Armenian youth who joined the Armenian Legion in the United States," and recreated from the original printing of a 1922 publication of the Armenian National Union. At the time of the article, the French military were searching their archives in France for additional or more complete information. The men's names were followed by their hometown village of birth and the city of residence in the U.S. The article was prefaced with, "Was your father or grandfather a Gamavor?" These were them. A list of all who had volunteered from this country. One column listed hometowns.

I did not know about the Gamavor before then. I naturally scanned the list looking for mentions of Kessab. First, I found some familiar names—Giragosian, Misak; Messerian, Serop, etc. Then, unexpectedly came two names that caught my breath: Boghos Boghossian, Kessab, New York. And Asadour Karamardian, Kessab, Detroit.

"Asadour made it to America!" I screamed through my window. To find his name in print felt like coming upon lost treasure after a long search. Perhaps, he died in the war. Or, had gone to fight and then left Syria for South America after the war. This thought made sense. But I was mistaken in quickly assuming Asadour, Jido's long-lost brother, had fought in the war.

Aunt Mary in Tarzana, California, set me straight (two decades later). It was the cousin, not the brother. Jido's cousin Asadour had come to Michigan after his studies and enlisted with the Gamavor. Mary knew her father, Boghos, and Asadour had both also joined the Gamavor in Kessab after the war—the word representing the volunteer fighters who protected townsfolk from Turks who continued to attack the surrounding region. She gave me the photo, too, of that group from 1923, titled "Gamavor from 1923." Undoubtedly, Asadour, Boghos, and Khatchig Karamardian are all in the photo (though I do not know which faces identify them).

The First World War has captured the imagination of people around the world for over a century. Yet so little is known of its impact in the Middle East. I was exposed only by inhaling stories written by third-generation Armenians like me, who penned the firsthand accounts of marches, deaths, and survivals of grandparents. Henry Morganthau was Ambassador to Turkey throughout the war, and also penned a book that I suspect few have read. He chronicled horrors that he was hearing of, all the while sounding an alarm to deaf ears back home. Missionary accounts are isolated and typically limited to their organizations. School curriculum doesn't touch the areas beyond the western fronts of Europe. The public has been exposed to little more than a slice of cinematic warfare in the classic film, *Lawrence of Arabia*.

The relatives in California, my Karamardian discoveries—those people who connect me from the past to the present—told me about the shoes. The family trade of shoemaking, the red *Yemeni* shoes that were their trademark product, the Yemeni shoes that her Uncle Khatchig made for Aunt Mary in his shoe shop in Kessab. There were shoe shops in Kessab, in Kaladouran, and in Latakia. My mind filled with stories from other family groupings around shoe shops. For one thing, Uncles Leo and Archie had started off with a shoe shop in Detroit. It was the Detroit cousins who shared a story of how the brothers, including Jido, had met Martha's future husband in a shoe shop; how they had arranged to introduce the couple.

"You come back here next week," they said to Gazar Karagozian. "Our sister comes from Beyruth. We bring her."

For the Karamardian family, the shoe shop was like the neighborhood barbershop of America—a social gathering place for male community. That bastion of male sociability clearly morphed anew, in the transition to modern American life. I witnessed it myself, this new sacred place—the living room card table! Once I gathered the threads and began to sort them into a life story, I could see that the games of cards paralleled, and ultimately replaced, the shoe shop. Pinochle (or poker) became the social center of Jido's life and those of his various communities.

Decades after I met the Karamardians in Los Angeles, my cousin Sossi introduced me to the world of Kessab through living relatives. I was able to absorb something of life in Kessab from Boghos' daughters Mary and Armine (Sossi's mother and aunt). Armine had come in 1949, driven across country from New York to L.A. after first visiting my grandparents at the farm (and also spent time in Martha's kitchen with Mary, Martha, and the two Alices.) Sossi, her sister and her mother, Mary, held court at their home while a number of people introduced as Kessabtsis stopped by regularly. And Sossi was vigilant with suggestions of people I should meet who were, in some way, "Karamardian." I met Kerop Kazozian, who described memories of his grandfather Khatchig on the march and the camp at Port Said. His mother was one of five daughters (six children total) of Khatchig, the very household that had welcomed Alice home from Turkey in 1925. Sossi also encouraged me to visit the widow of Vahan (Alice's brother) in Paris, France, Rosa Karamardian, who had killed her husband in 1950, within the passionate chaos of a domestic dispute. (She opened up another Armenian world of occupied France during the second war, a tale for another volume).

By this time, I was familiar with the organization called KEA and the annual yearbook on our coffee tables titled "Kessabtsis in the United States and Canada." I knew it was centered in Los Angeles. Sossi took me to the Kessab Educational Center on a Wednesday night, card night (naturally), to meet more relatives. In particular, she wanted me to meet Khatchig Titizian, who had recently moved to Yerevan, Armenia and was visiting L.A. that week. Khatchig provided to me the survival story of his grandmother, Shoushan Karamardian Titizian, one more of my grandfather's cousins.

Besides the loss of two children, her deportation group had been fortunate to have spent most of the war in Amman, Jordan, under British control, where Shoushan had cooked for the refugee camp and safely returned to Kessab with her family mostly intact (the exceptions were teenaged daughter, Frieda, who had died at the camp plus an infant had died on the march). When we met, Shoushan had just passed, at well beyond one hundred years old. (I had been told about her a decade before, when she was already known as the oldest woman in Kessab. And her husband lived to 108). Her story stood out as the only lucky one among our tribe, which was itself of significance to me. But my skin prickled with goosebumps when her grandson pointed out a heartbreaking detail: Shoushan's camp in Jordan stands the same today, over one hundred years later. The very same camp is still home to millions of refugees!

It was what Khatchig did next that would haunt me for the remainder of my life. He reached up to the bookshelves that lined the center's walls and pulled down a book, telling me it contained the only census ever recorded in Kessab and its villages. It was printed in 1911. My great grandfather's immediate family were living then in Latakia, and therefore not included in the Kessab census. Khatchig explained that numerous other Karamardians would not be counted because many had migrated over the Turkish border to Iskenderun (known now as Alexandretta). Evidently, at the time, work was scarce in Kessab and many of its people found work there. Khatchig he did not read out the whole census or even from all the villages of Kessab. But he did read, and translate for me, the names of all Karamardians that were listed in both Kaladouran and in Kessab proper.

Until that moment, I had been carrying a file in my head, titled "1915." To Armenians the world over, "1915" holds a significance I can best describe as what "9/11" means to any Americans over the age of thirty. Both of these numbers represent a moment in history where whole societies realize that their future, and that of future generations, will never again feel as it had prior to that particular year. The last century kicked off a war in which the first human genocide was hidden from the public, other than the witness testimony of some missionaries and one ambassador. Rather than correct course, it marched on to an even greater evil cloaked within a second world war. Races of people continued to die because Hitler, famous for his retort to advisors who questioned his plans for the Jews, said, "Whoever remembers the Armenians today?" Such impunity rumbled along, in spite of cries of "never again!" to ring in the next century, the one we currently find ourselves in, with yet more senseless war choices and increased violence around the world. Worst of all, victims' pain from violence is only enhanced by denials—Holocaust deniers, denial of genocide by governments—or convenient choices to ignore. A new date pushed its way into my dreams to haunt me. The photos from 1911 verified the very people whose stories I sought, whose existence I knew of. And now, a single census list—the only one—proved…verified the existence of the "forgotten ones."

Less than one third of the Armenian population of the Ottoman Empire survived the genocide. I scan a list of family in one village and one town center and count six survivors. Using this model alone, the math informs me that the Karamardian family fared worse than the 30% survival rate.

I have memorized this list, frantically written out in my sloppy hand, over the years since. I typed and printed it, study it regularly, and find myself just staring and contemplating. A few names I recognized immediately from characters I know. Elisa (Aunt Alice) aged six, her little brother Vahan, one year old; Asadour, cousin to my grandfather whose name was undoubtedly recorded before he went to New York to study, listed here with his family; Sossi's grandfather, Serop, with his family unit, Shoushan Titizian and possibly her parents next door, Khatchig… These are the very few survivors. I know them now, have even met most of them, know their personalities, know their stories, have recorded their stories.

When I had first met the Karamardians in 1977, a group clustered around tables calling out details and conferring amongst themselves as they helped me sketch out a loose family tree. Every time they mentioned a name I had scrawled, then casually added "he died" or "she died in the war," I hastily scratched an asterisk after the name. But this list fills in more names—complete families that had been, and then were no more.

Those other names? I stare and blink. I discover that Aunt Alice had also a little sister named Vartouhi. I search frantically for the worn pieces of paper containing my most precious treasures; both are letters written in response to my father's request for information, and each lays out the personal ordeal of a female victim in a matter-of-fact manner. One from Martha's daughter and dictated by Martha; the other from Alice herself. The letter that Alice wrote to my father told her story in a brief, perfunctory way: how an aunt called out to her to say her father was in the army, how she was taken to the orphanage by train and given other names and cried, how she had seen her brother only briefly—when moved to a new orphanage, how priests came to give them back their names, how she chose to stay and study after the war, until Kamal took power and it was no longer safe. I was mostly taken by her decisions as a young girl all alone in the world, decisions that revolved around education, as if learning for her was like bread to others trying to survive starvation in the camps across the Ottomon world. Her letter mentions Vahan, the little brother, whose story I chased to Paris, where he had lived as a tailor. His tragic story is too dense to include in this book. But Alice made no mention of Vartouhi, who is clearly another sibling on the census list. Neither does she mention her parents. I wonder, did she fear talking about the dead? Was that a custom, perhaps a survival technique? Maybe it just wasn't relevant to the facts she was laying out in the moment. After all, she was an educated woman offering pertinent information.... in this case, of the living.

Vartouhi was no more, like all these other names. All but the six survivors of Jido's generation that I am now familiar with—these remaining names document some of the dead. Killed, or died on the marches. The victims. In short, the 1911 census of Kessab is a list of dead family. Family who, by the end of 1915, no longer existed. Victims of Medz Yeghern (the great evil crime).

This story of humankind was no longer distant, no longer a vague concept of a long ago time. This, like the horrors of Jim Crow I had learned as a teen—this was close to home. These were great grandparents, great aunts, uncles, cousins. The lost ones.

Forever silent.

May God rest their souls.

Kessab Boys to Study, likely graduation photo

Front row left to right: Boghos (Paul/Ingles) Boghossian, Asadour Karamardian (of Giragos)

Back row left to right: Churukian brother, Boujikian (nickname Khasir), Josef Churukian

Freedom Fighters of Kessab (post-war Gamavor)
in Kaladouran 1923

First Generation in new world circa 1918

Left to right: John Peter, Albert Simon, Jacob Peter, Zaha Peter (the first)*

*deceased approximately 3 years old

First Schoolhouse (at King and Danby Rds)
Four Peter children

Bottom left, Susie; third from bottom left, Mitch; behind Mitch, Jake; right with glasses, John

Farmer Joe Peter

Bedros Line

BEDROS KARAMARDIAN AND TZAGHIR INJEJIKIAN

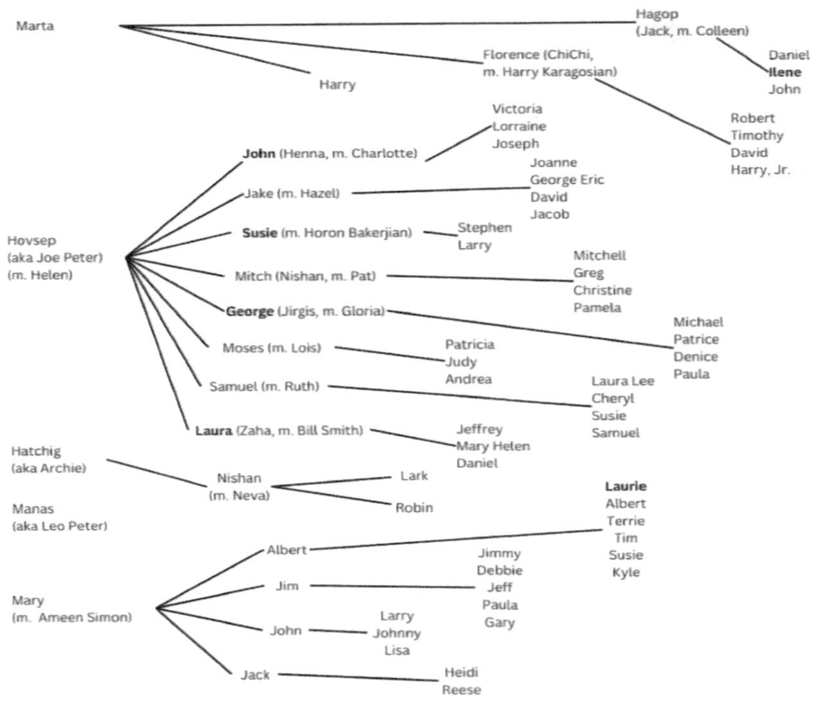

Marta
  Harry
  Florence (ChiChi, m. Harry Karagosian)
    Victoria
    Lorraine
    Joseph
  Hagop (Jack, m. Colleen)
    Daniel
    Ilene
    John
    Robert
    Timothy
    David
    Harry, Jr.

Hovsep (aka Joe Peter) (m. Helen)
  John (Henna, m. Charlotte)
    Joanne
    George Eric
    David
    Jacob
  Jake (m. Hazel)
    Stephen
    Larry
  Susie (m. Horon Bakerjian)
    Mitchell
    Greg
    Christine
    Pamela
  Mitch (Nishan, m. Pat)
    Patricia
    Judy
    Andrea
  George (Jirgis, m. Gloria)
    Michael
    Patrice
    Denice
    Paula
  Moses (m. Lois)
    Laura Lee
    Cheryl
    Susie
    Samuel
  Samuel (m. Ruth)
    Jeffrey
    Mary Helen
    Daniel
  Laura (Zaha, m. Bill Smith)

Hatchig (aka Archie)
  Nishan (m. Neva)
    Lark
    Robin

Manas (aka Leo Peter)
  Albert
    Laurie
    Albert
    Terrie
    Tim
    Susie
    Kyle
  Jim
    Jimmy
    Debbie
    Jeff
    Paula
    Gary

Mary (m. Ameen Simon)
  John
    Larry
    Johnny
    Lisa
  Jack
    Heidi
    Reese

GLOSSARY
NAMES, PLACES AND THINGS IN ODAR WITH VARIOUS SPELLINGS

Amirka; (pronunciation for America by first generation Armenians)

Kessab, Kasap, Kesap, Casab, Casbis; town northwesternmost in Syria, on Turkish border, until years was exclusively, and is still predominantly, Armenian; named Casabelle and Casabella by first Crusaders

Latakia, Lattakia, Ladehkiya
 (Kessabtsi pronunciation), Al Ladhiqiyah Port City in Northwest Syria; ancient name Laodice

Kaladouran, Karadouran; coastal village of Kessab, northwest Syria on border with Turkey

Beirut, Beyruth, Beyrout; major city in Lebanon

Tartus, Tartous

Junieh, Jounieh

Port Hune (pronunciation of Port Huron by first generation Syrians, Armenians) in Michigan, U.S.

Itaka, Ithaca (pronunciation by Joe Peter) in Finger Lakes region of New York on Cayuga Lake

J'abal A'qra, Jebbel Akra, Mount Cassius; mountain of Kessab

Jabal Mussa, Musa Dagh, Kizil Dagh; name for mountain and village of and near Kessab

Iskenderun, Alexandretta; (modern name) city in Turkey near border of Syria

Aintab; Gaziantep (Turkish name)

Constantinople; Istanbul (modern name)

Melkia, B'Melki, kfar melki; costal village near Lebanon (residents called themselves Syrian circa 1900)

Barlum Monastery, Ballum, Barlahoy, Barlaam; (believed to be founded by St. Barlaam)

Legion d'Orient, Armenian Leggionaires, Gamavor; names for the group of Armenian fighters WW1

Gamavor; volunteers, freedom fighters in Kessab after the war who patrolled and protected Kessab area

Shushan, Shoushan (Lily, name in Armenian and Hebrew)

Elisa, Alice

Armine, Armenouhi, (Armen, male version)

Asadour, Asadur

Ameen (family spelling), Amin (usual Arabic spelling)

Bedros, Boutris, Bete, Peter; Armenian, Greek, Arabic, English versions

Hovsep, Youssef, Youssif, Jose, Joseph, Joe; Armenian, Arabic, Spanish, English versions

Khatchig, Hatchig, Archie

Boghos, Paul

Laura, Zaha, Zahia, Zahea, Florence (meaning flower, Arabic versions)

Henna, Hana, John

Manas, Manasse, Leo

Moses, Mose, Mussa, Moussa, Moosey (nickname in Peter family)

Marta, Martha

Mary, Mariam, Maryam

Louise, Louisa, Louiza, Lousine

Nishan, Nishon, Mitchell

George, Giragos (Armenian), Jirgis (Syrian)

Yunnus, Younus, Yunus (Arabic) Yunis (Greek)

Tzaghir, Dzaghir, Tsaghig, Kitcha, Haigha, Zarig, Zaghig; (meaning flower, Armenian version female)

Kamor, Ataturk; 1923 took control as leader of Turkey

Kibbe, kibbee, kibbeh, kufta (Armenian version); baked mix of lamb with pine nuts and bulgar

Lubi, loobi; green bean and tomato stew, usually with chunks of lamb

Lamajoun, lamajoon, Lahmajoun; meat pies on flat bread made with ground meat, onions and peppers

Koussa, kousa, cusa (squash, zucchini, usually stuffed with meat and rice)

Babagnoush, babaganoush (eggplant)

Shadiyeh; Arabic word for pilaf

Shankleesh, tchingleesh; a cheese spiced and coated with zatar, a middle Eastern spice

Sourkig, Armenian pizza

Dolma, dolmades (Greek) tolma, sarma (Armenian); rolled grapeleaves, stuffed with meat and rice

Pigegh; Armenian olive oil bread twisted in knot shapes

Baklava, paklava; type of pastry layers with nuts and syrup, cut into diamond shapes

Boorma; version of baklava with nuts and syrup inside rolled pastry layers and cut in cigar shapes

Smeed; pastry cake made with farina

Hayrig; Armenian for father

Mayrig; Armenian for mother

Jihdo, Jido, Jid, Jidi; Arabic for grandfather, my grandfather (our version Jido)

Jida, Jidehti, Sito; Arabic for grandmother (our version, Sito)

Shukran, shookran; Arabic for thank you

Yallah, yella; Arabic for come on, let's go

Kee-fek, kee-fik; Arabic hello

Huffla, mahrajan; Syrian festival

Effendi; man of education in Ottoman Empire

Gendarme; officer of authority, such as police

Tonir; oven

Odar; Armenian for "other, stranger, foreigner"

Jan; a term of endearment in Armenian, i.e. Louisa-jan or Stepan Jan (i.e. Louisa, dear)

Inch bes es?; Armenian for How are you?

Shad lav em, park asdouzo; Armenian for I am fine, thank you.

Barev; Armenian for Hello

Medz Yeghern; "Great Evil Crime" (Armenian)

Last names connected to or associated with Karamardian family: Injejikian, Aslanian, Giragossian, Chalakian, Margosian, Karagozian, Karagosian, Titizian, M'gerditchian, Boghossian, Churukian, Sarkissian, Apelian, Terterian, Ashekian, Nazarian, Kakusian, Asarian, Hasessian, Ayanian, Berber

BIBLIOGRAPHY AND RECOMMENDED READING

Arlen, Michael J. *Passage to Ararat*. Farrar, Strauss and Giroux, 1975.

Balakian, Peter. *The Black Dog of Fate*. Basic Books, 1997.

Balakian, Peter. *The Burning Tigris: The Armenian Genocide and America's Response*. Harper Collins, 2003.

Bohjalian, Chris. *Sandcastle Girls*. Knopf Doubleday Publishing Group, 2013.

Edgarian, Carol. *Rise the Euphrates*. Random House, 1994.

Hovannisian, Richard G. *The Republic of Armenia, Volumes 1 – 4*. Univ. of California Press, 1971.

Hovannisian, Richard G. *Armenian People from Ancient to Modern Times Vols I and II*. Palgrave MacMillan US, 1997.

Kessab Educational Association. *Kessab and the Kessabtsis: Special edition commemorating 50th anniversary*. KEA of LA, Calif, USA, 2011.

Marcom, Micheline Aharonian. *Three Apples Fell From Heaven, A Novel.* Riverhead Books, a member of Penguin Putnam, Inc., 2001.

Mouradian, Khatchig. *Resistance Network: The Armenian Genocide and Humanitarianism in Ottoman Syria 1915-1918.* Michigan State University Press, 2021.

Morganthau, Henry. *Ambassador Morganthau's Story; A Personal Account of the Armenian Genocide.* Original publish date 1918. Reprinted with Edwin Mellen Press, 2022.

Pattie, Susan Paul. *The Armenian Legionnaires: Sacrifice and Betrayal in WWI.* I.B. Tauris, 2018.

Sanjian, Avedis. *Armenian Communities in Syria under Ottoman Dominion.* Harvard University Press, 1965.

Sarkissian, Hagop. *From Kessab to Watertown: A Modern Saga.* Ohan Press, 1966.

Werfel, Frantz. *The Forty Days of Musa Dagh.* Fischer Verlag, translate David R. Godine, 1933.

Online resources

100 Years of Reformed Presbyterian Missions in Syria: Part 1 of 2 retrieved from Gentlereformation.com

Various entries retrieved from Presbyterianmission.org

Author Unknown (2015, August, 12) The Dominican Republic and its Arab Assimilation. Retrieved from Abreu Report: Global Politics.

Unpublished

George Peter. *Karamardian Kapers - personal journal writings.*

Laura Peter Smith. Various letters, 1942-1947.

NOTE ON FICTION AND TRUTH

The ***Odar*** series is a work of fiction, though based on true events, true people, and mostly authentic attitude and personality. I seem to have exhausted (of my ability and to my knowledge) access to information through documented research. And I have incorporated most of what I gratefully received through first, second and third hand interviews. Yet, I fully expect additional detail to appear after publication of this work; perhaps via relatives as yet unknown to me, perhaps from less likely sources or from completely unexpected windfall. After many decades of searching and processing clues and details, nothing would surprise me.

For all the factual detail existing in *Odar*, I found it most feasible to fully share the story of Joe Peter and the settling of his several communities during historic times as a work of fiction, in order to best see the members of one family in all their human thought and action. Imagination served for certain details of action, plot and character development – gaps filled in, opinions, thoughts, and sentiments assigned. There is no way to share the material facts in my possession without some guesswork as to the heart at the center of them. I sincerely hope not to cause inconvenience to any living person via my method or for any error I may have inadvertently ascribed to real people through the telling.

I have not changed names in this story. In fact, I have taken the liberty to include real names and places gleaned from census records, passenger lists, naturalization applications, and other available documentation and assign them roles. I chose to insert real people into the lives of my ancestors where I deemed the association likely and logical, or heard mention of said persons in interviews or through family folklore. Since this telling is about real people and real places, I found little reason to fabricate in cases where names are available on record.

Finally, to quote author Yiyun Li (The New Yorker, Oct 30, 2023): "Some fiction is tamer than some life…"

I could not have expressed in a better way, the end result of the story I have laid out in these pages. Naturally, there is more than a little family drama that I have omitted. Family folklore or secrets unearthed by accident tend to exist within the fabric of most families. In this case, certain sensational details, of murder and mayhem, may well deserve their own storyline in a full volume, while detracting from this one. So yes, this work of fiction may be somewhat tamer than the complete unabridged life of Joseph Peter and/or the greater Karamardian family. But this is the story I have chosen to tell. I hope, and believe, it is enough. And that the reader has gained from the telling.

Most importantly, I dedicate this series to all of my family and to families everywhere, in all their glory and complication. And to the memory of all ancestors.

Denice Peter Karamardian

GRATITUDE RUNS DEEP

There are few words for the depth of my feelings for the primary angels of this project. First and foremost, my inspiration, my collaborator and connecting thread, a primary voice and soulmate in the journey – my late father, **George Peter,** who talked and wrote about his life and helped to access and interview first generation major characters in the book, his aunts. I dedicate every word to him, in absentia. I hope he is enjoying eternal space with the others, and the ancestors.

Sossi (Karamardian) Madzounian, my angel guide, facilitated my search and discovery with hospitality beyond belief, directed me far and wide, introduced me to the Kessab community in L.A. and continually inspires me, along with her entire family. *Ilene Karagozian Hill,* my inaugural host/guide who helped me launch discovery with graciousness, care and interest. *Lisa Bennett,* my first editor, helped shape a story line from dense quantity of material into a first draft with patience and mind blowing guidance and wisdom.

The storytellers were crucial blessings in my life to the endeavor. As witnesses, they evolved into the major character and storytellers of Odar. Their words reached out, some from final days on a sofa, others from the great beyond, to shape the world and challenges they had known and overcome: **Marta Karamardian Karagozian, Alice Karamardian Margosian, Serop Karamardian, Louisa Guzelian Karamardian, ChiChi (Florence) Karagosian, and Dr. Vahan Churukian.**

(The females listed here spoke in absentia.) Their stories were augmented (and some narrated) by **Mary Boghossian Karamardian, Armine Boghossian Thomson, Seta Der Terossian Karamardian Soma, Stepan Karamardian, and Madame Rosa Karamardian**. Profound witnessing over many decades, which shaped much of the narration for the story of Odar, came from closer to home: **John Peter, Susie Peter Bakerjian, and Laura Peter Smith** (my father's siblings).

All of the above have deceased since my interviews with them. So too, have some of the second generation witnesses who provided in depth information and enhanced experience: **Gabriel Injejikian, Neva Karamardian, Harry Karagosian, Colleen Karagozian,** Cat, **Barbara and Lorraine Abraham**. I am so very grateful for the sharing of their memories of old world childhoods from *Garbis Karamardian, Anoush Karamardian Tohikian, and Kerop Kazarian*. And then of course, more miraculously appearing relatives with revelations: *Khatchig Titizian, Laurie Cunnington and the Simon sisters*.

There was much additional help from ....*Gary Lind-Sinanian* - curator, Armenian Library and Museum of America, Watertown, MA.; *Makda Watherspoon* of Cornell Arabic Department for document translations; *Kessab Educational Center*, Los Angeles, CA; *Carol Kammen*, historian, for an Ithaca initiation to research; *Lansing Historical Society and Salt Point Park exhibit*; *Peter Balakian*, author, for trailblazing guidance, research, and inspiration; my French translators in Paris, France *Nicholas Karamardian, Karim Bachiri, and Nadea; Jana Hextor*, medium; the *Cornell Armenian Student Association*, language classes and social support.

A very special shout out to *Steven Manley* for graphic support, *Jeffrey Smith*, for technical design (map) and technical support (photos), and once again to the very talented Sossi Madzounian for cover art (photographic for all jacket covers).

I'm grateful for additional support from cousins: *Dan and John Karagozian, Larry Bakerjian, Lark Karamardian, Alice Karamardian Vartabedian, Elo Tohikian,* and *Liza Karamardian Carter.* Also *Leslie Daniels,* author, for helpful advice and a first look at book content, *Alison Wearing,* (Stratford, Canada) memoire instructor, and my very patient friend and early copy editor, *Donna Ramer.*

Thank you to more **editors**: *Kate Allyson, Brian Dooley, Ashley Swanson.* **Last, but never least**, **early readers and cheerleaders**......*Mary Helen Myrdek, Paula Peter, Vally Kovary, Maureen Moore, Vicky Hutchinson, Michael J. Peter, Daniel Terino, Donna Ramer,* and *Patrice DiLorenzo.*

Note: names in bold represent deceased participants

ABOUT THE AUTHOR

Photo by T.C. Peter

Denice Peter Karamardian owns and operates a regional publication for Finger Lakes wine visitors and is at work on several books. She is retired from a rich tapestry of overlapping careers that spanned over forty plus years and included instructing voice, host/producer of radio concert broadcast series, fifty years of music and theater performance, columnist and reviewer. She currently lives in her hometown of Ithaca, New York (where she operated a bed and breakfast for two decades) near/with her family.

www.ingramcontent.com/pod-product-compliance
Lightning Source LLC
Chambersburg PA
CBHW020655060526
44119CB00090B/393/J